Thanks You
Ahmad for all
of your assistance

Joe

NIMBLE BOOKS LLC

The Definitive Illustrated History of the Torpedo Boat (The Ship Killers) by Joe Hinds

Volume 1: Overview

Volume 2: Timeline 1280–1899

Volume 3: Timeline 1900–August 1939

Volume 4: Timeline September 1939–1940

Volume 5:Timeline 1941

Volume 6:Timeline 1942

Volume 7:Timeline 1943

Volume 8:Timeline 1944

Volume 9:Timeline 1945

Volume 10: Appendices, Index, and Never-Before-Published Bonus Images

Complete set available as a unit in January 2010 (ISBN 978-1-934840-58-0)

If you would like to contribute a future volume to The Ship Killers, *please contact the series editor, Joe Hinds, at* Joe.Hinds@gmail.com, *or the publisher, Fred Zimmerman, at* wfz@NimbleBooks.com. *Information about writing for Nimble Books is available under "Publish With Us" at www.NimbleBooks.com.*

THE SHIP KILLERS

A DEFINITIVE HISTORY OF THE TORPEDO BOAT

VOLUME 2: TIMELINE 1280–1899

BY JOE HINDS

NIMBLE BOOKS LLC

NIMBLE BOOKS LLC

CONTENTS

Figures

DEDICATION

Joe Judge, Curator Hampton Roads Naval Museum Joe has spent the best part of nine years proofing my work,. He has helped me find research resources, mounted a full blown art show for my work and spending endless hours, at home, correcting my infantile spelling and grammar errors. Joe has always had words of encouragement when I hit low ebb. You, the reader, would not be reading this but for Joe Judge.

A GLOBAL TIMELINE OF THE TORPEDO BOAT

The title says it all. This is, I believe, the first truly global view of the history of the torpedo boat. This is a fascinating piece of naval history that, in my view, has never been examined in a a systematic, comprehensive, global and detailed fashion. There are hundreds of books on MTB's, PT's, MAS boast, and S boats. The cover usually carries a speeding something flashing across the cover leaving a huge wake and photos of valiant young men with death grips on machine guns. That describes about 95% of the small war-boat books out there. I have looked on these with great interest but I also put down each book with the thoughts, "Why were they important? What did they contribute to victory or defeat? How did the design evolve?" And I had hundreds of other unanswerable questions.

I set out in 1999 to produce a set of illustrations depiction the overall evolution of the torpedo boat. I had to dig in the most obscure documents to find the origin of designs, the story's of successes and failures and the most difficult part-the colors of the boats. I purchased sixty sets of torpedo boat plans and four came with color information. My illustration of the Type S-100 boat took two years to nail down the exact color mix that the i used. I spent another two years hunting down information of the CSS *David*, the first military model of a spar-torpedo boat.

In the beginning, I stored research material in 3" thick 3-ring binders and in the first year, I had filled three. I now have twenty-five binders and enough material for another ten 3-ring binders. I had to stop buying books after my first one-hundred and went to the best source in the world, the Interlibrary Loan Service from our state library. I have scanned a good part of over 300 books and I still run across information I have never seen before.

The idea for displaying the sequential history of the torpedo bat came from a man named Lieutenant G.E. Armstrong, RN, 1896, in his book *Torpedoes and Torpedo-Vessels*. In the back of Armstrong's book is a tabular listing on events in the development of the, torpedo boats, mines, and underwater explosive devices, up to his time. It was through this style of tracking information that I learned of a torpedo vessel I had never heard of before, John Ericsson's, "*Destroyer.*" It turns out that there are a great many MTB enthusiasts who had also never heard of it. What became clear from Armstrong's work was the importance of these boats in naval matters of his time. The design evolution became quite clear. The shift from spar-torpedo to Whitehead's "Fish" torpedo was evident.

The book has been separated into ten volumes. As the reader progresses through the timelines in this and the following volumes, he can see the obvious differences between those navies who maximized the Motor Torpedo Boat and those who neglected it. It becomes glaringly clear that as the war advanced, the need for the motor torpedo boat grew ever more important. This fact becomes more evident in 1944 when the world wide use of the torpedo boat was on a par with air forces and armies of tanks.

This is not a book of endless lists, I was never after collecting massive amounts of data to list every boat ever built. I was not after yet another set of lists that showed only torpedo boats sunk. There are over 1,000 small stories of individual actions, fleet actions, accidents and events of stupendous valor performed by torpedo boat men. Many of these events are only eight words long and some are maybe thirty words long, yet I hope that none of them is without interest. The collective work shows the full scope of this missing piece of naval history.

This whole story loops back to relevance in our world today. In 2000, the destroyer *USS Cole* was almost sunk by a small boat manned by desperate men. In 2007, Iranian navy sent out small speedboats to taunt the British navy in the Gulf of Oman and embarrassed a world power to near tears. In 2009, navies of every nation are being embarrassed by pirates in the Gulf of Aden. Once again, men in small boats are proving the limited power of "Big" ships with "Big" guns in shallow waters. Funny how the lessons of history are constantly being taught.

NIMBLE BOOKS LLC

TIMELINE 1280–1899

Date	Craft, Name, Event or Country	Event, Builder and Boat Specifications	City, River, Lake, Sea, Ocean
1280	al-Rammah Water-Borne Surface Torpedo	The works of Syrian military engineer Hasan Al-Rammah, called "Najm-al-Din" (Star of the Faith), have been well known for hundreds of years, but it is only recently that his efforts and achievements have been fully understood in the West. Al-Rammah explained and perfected the recipes for several types of explosive gunpowder. He was very adept at explaining the fundamentals of high-grade gunpowder by purification processes for potassium nitrate, a key ingredient in high grade gunpowder. [95] [96] Several scholars have reached the conclusion that one of the devices al-Rammah designed was intended to be a torpedo.[97] [98] The significance of this new information about al-Rammah is that it moves back the origin of torpedoes and naval explosive devices by more than three hundred years to a different continent and a different civilization. Now the record is corrected and history can be formally amended.	Syria during the Mamluk dynasty

---

[95] Ahmad Y. Al-Hassan and Donald R. Hill, *Islamic Technology: An Illustrated History* (Cambridge: Cambridge University Press and UNESCO, 1986, paperback, 1992) and Al-Hassan, *History of Science and Technology in Islam*, http://ww.history-science-technology.com.

[96] Professor Mohammed Mansour, Foundation for Science Technology and Civilization, U.K.

[97] J.R. Partington, *History of Greek Fire and Gunpowder*, (Baltimore: The John Hopkins University Press, 1999) "... has been supposed to be a torpedo."

[98] Willy Ley, *Rockets, Missiles and Space Travel* (New York: The Viking Press, 1958): "But Hasan Al-Rammah added one unsuspected novelty: a rocket-propelled torpedo..."

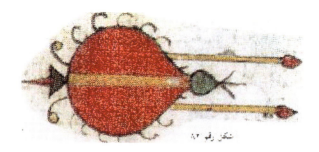

Figure 1. al-Rammah torpedo. The pear-shaped vessel , made from sheet-iron, was filled with gunpowder and incendiary materials. One or more rockets were used for propelling it towards its target. The long rods acted like rudders and helped to steer the torpedo. (Ahmad Y. al-Hassan)

Figure 2. A conceptual model of the floating torpedo describved by Hasan al-Rammah, created by FSTC Ltd. (Foundation for Science and Technology, Ltd.)

Date	Craft, Name, Event or Country	Event, Builder and Boat Specifications	City, River, Lake, Sea, Ocean
1585[99]	Siege of Antwerp "Eighty Years War"	Small boat warfare among European navies began here, with Italian engineer Frederico Gianibelli at the siege of Antwerp. He had to remove enemy forces from a bridge over the river Scheldt. His two small skiffs, loaded with many barrels of gunpowder and covered with marble gravestones, were sent drifting down the river as with a clockwork mechanism for the fuse ticking away. At the bridge, the explosive force of the boats sent marble shrapnel flying against the 2400-foot-long bridge killed 800 soldiers of the Duke of Parma, Alessandro Farnese, and blew a hole 200 feet wide through the barricade on the bridge.	River Scheldt
1624[100]	1620-1624 Cornelius Van Drebbel Submarine Boat	Van Drebbel used designs from William Bourne, 1578, to make the earliest known European navigable submarine boat. Van Drebbel performed several successful dives at depths of 12 to 15 feet. He made three test vessels, the last capable of carrying 16 people and powered by six oars. This model was demonstrated to King James I as well as several thousand onlookers. The submarine stayed submerged for three hours and traveled between Westminster and Greenwich.	Thames River, England
1627[101]	Van Drebbel's Floating Petard	King James commissioned Van Drebbel to set up shop and manufacture "Floating Petards" for use by the British Navy to break the French blockade of La Rochelle. They were unsuccessful and were determined to be a greater danger to the British than to the French.	La Rochelle, France
1730[102]	John T. Desaguliers Underwater Rocket Torpedo	The inventor made several successful tests sinking small boats on with underwater explosive rockets.	Plymouth, England

---

[99] Sleeman, 330.

[100] *Ibid.*

[101] *Ibid.*

[102] *Ibid.*

Figure 3. The Eighty Years War. The Liberation of Antwerp. (Museum of Antwerp).

Figure 4. The emblem of the Dutch "Sea Beggars." The Dutch fought against
Spanish occupation from 1550 to 1583. The Sea Beggars legend still lives on in
Dutch folk lore as privateers, pirates, patriots and thieves. (Museum of
Antwerp)

Figure 5. This scanned postcard shows a popular and mythical representation of Drebbel's diving boat.

Figure 6. BBC sponsored a team to build a reproduction of the real Drebbel craft after years of careful research. The full size operating model is on display at Heron Square, Richmond on the Thames. ("Gunner54" on Wordpress.com, used with permission.)

Date	Craft, Name, Event or Country	Event, Builder and Boat Specifications	City, River, Lake, Sea, Ocean
1774[103]	Mr. Day Diving Boat	An eager inventor who made two test runs with his "Diving Boat." On the second run, the boat and inventor stayed on the bottom.	Plymouth, England
1775[104]	Captain David Bushnell	Leaning on the history of the efforts of European inventors, David Bushnell made several successful experiments exploding charges of gunpowder underwater.	New York Harbor
1776[105]	Sgt. Ezra Lee *Turtle*	The American diving boat *Turtle,* driven by Sergeant Lee, attempted to attack and sink the British ship *HMS Eagle* in New York harbor. The unwieldy craft and lack of oxygen almost killed the sergeant.	New York Harbor
1777[106]	Capt. D. Bushnell *Turtle*	Bushnell went after the prize vessel *HMS Cerberus* with his newly created "Drifting Torpedoes." The torpedo was caught by crewmembers aboard a prize schooner astern the *Cerberus*. Here, the mine exploded killing three crewmen and destroying a small boat onboard.	New London
1778[107]	January 6 Caleb Carman 'Battle of the Kegs'	The "Drifting Mines" made by Caleb Carman, were truly effective devices. Several barrels of gunpowder were fitted with a flintlock-firing device sensitive enough to set off the mine once it touched a ship. The British fleet anchored in the middle of the Delaware River and moved during the night into Philadelphia harbor to avoid being trapped in ice. One of the mines struck a small bridge and exploded killing four sailors and wounding several more.	Philadelphia Delaware River

---

[103] *Ibid.*

[104] *Ibid.*

[105] *Ibid.*

[106] *Ibid.*

[107] Sleeman, 330, and Battle of the Kegs <http://www.carman.net/battleofkegs.htm> and Evarts and Peck, *History of Burlington County,* 463.

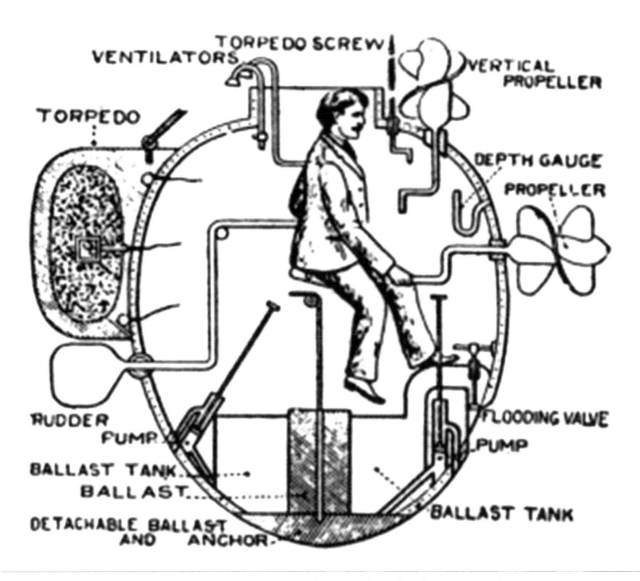

Figure 7. The best known illustration of the *Turtle*. Officially, America's first torpedo boat. (Library Of Congress Prints and Photographs Division)

Date	Craft, Name, Event or Country	Event, Builder and Boat Specifications	City, River, Lake, Sea, Ocean
1797[108]	Révéroni Saint Cyr Submarine Cannon	The French inventor proposed a catamaran hulled ship with a 48-pound carronade slung between the hulls and towed underwater.	France
1797[109]	Robert Fulton Torpedoes	Fulton turned from a career in art to science and weapons of war. His first fascination was with the concept of submarines and torpedoes. He had access to the works of both Saint Cyr and Drebbel and attempted to improve on their designs. Early torpedo experiments were largely monetary failures, but laid the groundwork for future trials.	France
1800[110]	July 24 Robert Fulton 'Nautilus'	His careful engineering and construction of the submarine *Nautilus* enabled Fulton to have many successful tests. This was the first known use of compressed air for breathing underwater. He could easily maneuver his submarine, maintained controlled descent and ascent, and could remain submerged for several hours with a "Snorkel"-type system.	Brest, Seine River, France
1801[111]	Robert Fulton Drifting Torpedo	This was the first successful experiment with a drifting torpedo. Fulton's efforts at exploding a torpedo against a small (40') vessel were successful. This is the first known event of a ship sunk by a "torpedo" from a distance (628 feet).	Brest France
1801[112]	Robert Fulton Drifting Torpedo	With the British and French at war, Fulton attempted to sink a British war ship with drifting torpedoes. The attack failed.	Boulogne France

---

[108] Sleeman, 330.

[109] *Ibid.*

[110] *Ibid.*

[111] Sleeman, 331.

[112] *Ibid.*

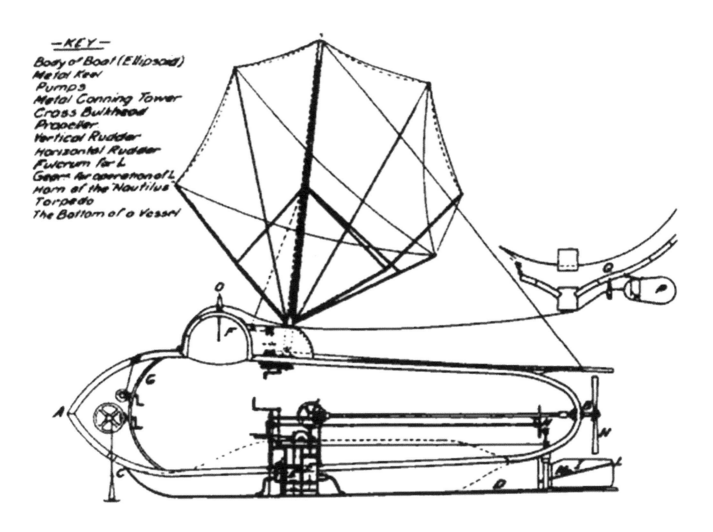

—KEY—
Body of Boat (Ellipsoid)
Metal Keel
Pumps
Metal Conning Tower
Cross Bulkhead
Propeller
Vertical Rudder
Horizontal Rudder
Fulcrum for L
Gear for operation of L
Horn of the "Nautilus"
Torpedo
The Bottom of a Vessel

Figure 8. A fully operational submarine. Fulton carried canisters of oxygen that enabled him to stay successfully submerged for hours. (Library Of Congress Prints and Photographs Division)

Date	Craft, Name, Event or Country	Event, Builder and Boat Specifications	City, River, Lake, Sea, Ocean
1804[113]	July 20 Robert Fulton Drifting Torpedo	After a falling out with the French naval authorities, Fulton sold his plans for "Underwater Bombs and other Aquatic devices" to the British Admiralty. His attack against the French fleet failed due to faulty construction. A torpedo exploded and caused no damage to any ship.	Boulogne France
1805[114]	Robert Fulton Drifting Torpedo	A second attempt that ended in failure. This was in part due to faulty construction and shoddy workmanship.	Boulogne France
1805[115]	Robert Fulton Drifting Torpedo	The old English brig *Dorothea* became the test vessel for further Fulton experiments with torpedoes. This time, two charges of 180 pounds of gunpowder with a clockwork-timed fuse blew up most dramatically.	Dover England
1807[116]	Robert Fulton Drifting Torpedo	Back in America, Fulton secured a large hulk from the Navy Department for a test of his torpedoes. He needed to several attempts before any of the torpedoes exploded against the ship.	New York
1810[117]	Robert Fulton Drifting Torpedo	The Navy scheduled Fulton to attempt an attack on the sloop *USS Argus*. At the test site, naval officers surrounded the vessel with netting and booms in a defensive position around the *Argus*. The attack failed as expected. Fulton was furious.	New York
1812[118]	Mr. Mix Drifting Torpedo	The inventor attempted an attack on *HMS Plantagenet* with several drifting torpedoes. All six attempts failed.	Lyn Haven Bay U.S.A.
1813[119]	Mr. Mix Drifting Torpedo	Mr. Mix next made a similar attack on *the HMS Ramilles* at harbor and failed. His drifting torpedo did destroy a schooner sitting alongside the target ship.	New York Harbor U.S.A.

---

[113] *Ibid.*

[114] *Ibid.*

[115] *Ibid.*

[116] *Ibid.*

[117] *Ibid.*

[118] *Ibid.*

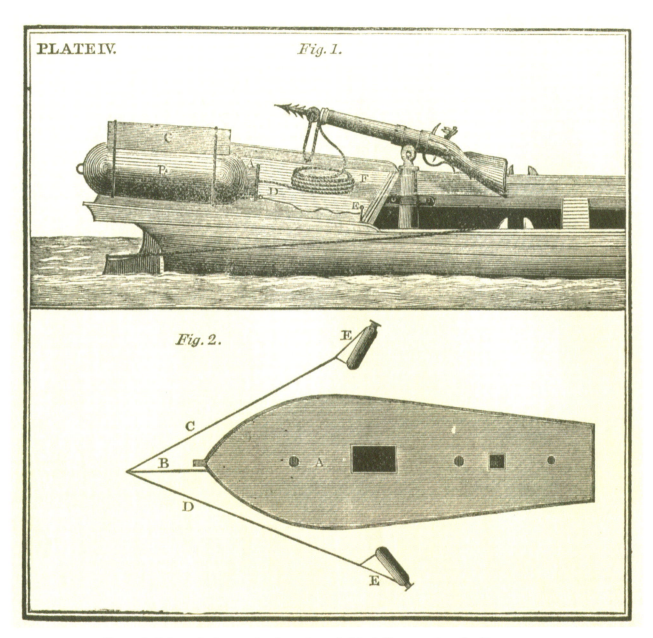

Figure 9. Fulton designs a simple and workable delivery system for his "Torpedoes." Once the harpoon struck an enemy ship the torpedo would be attached to the ships hull and the torpedo would be carried into the hull sinking the ship. (Library of Congress Prints and Photographs Division)

[119] *Ibid.*

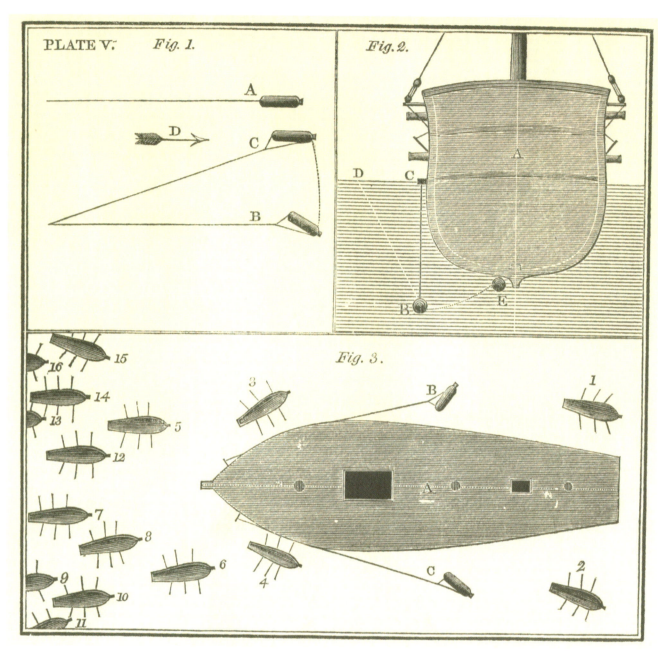

Figure 10. This shows how a fleet of small boats could attack and sink enemy ships in, rivers, harbors or estuaries. (Library of Congress Prints and Photographs Division)

Date	Craft, Name, Event or Country	Event, Builder and Boat Specifications	City, River, Lake, Sea, Ocean
1814[120]	Robert Fulton Submarine Gun	In New York harbor a replica of a ship's bulkhead attached to a raft became Fulton's target. Fulton's gun fired a shot that penetrated the test piece, which had the same thickness as a first-class ship of the line. He fired from between 12 and 15 feet of the target.	New York Harbor U.S.A.
1820[121]	Captain Johnson Submarine	Johnson's submarine carried its torpedo on its back. At the target ship, crewmembers would attach the torpedo to the bottom of the ship with screws. The trial was reported as successful but the Admiralty refused to sanction the vessel or torpedo. They declared it as too "diabolical."	Moulsford, Berks England
1826[122]	John Ericsson Sub-Aquatic Cannon	John Ericsson began to sketch ideas for a turreted war ship with his "Sub-Aquatic Cannons." He laid out the principles of a gun operated by a hydraulic and compressed air system. These ideas later became the *USS Monitor* and the torpedo ship *Destroyer*.	Sweden
1829[123]	July 4 Col. Samuel Colt Submarine Battery	Before Sam Colt was a known as a gun maker, he experimented with batteries, insulated copper wire, and underwater explosives. His torpedo (mine) destroyed a large raft on Ware Pond.	Ware Pond U.S.A.
1839[124]	Gen. Paisley, R. E. Submarine Torpedo	The general used a galvanic-firing device on his test against the HMS *Royal George.*[125] His test was successful.	Portsmouth, England

---

[120] *Ibid.*

[121] *Ibid.*

[122] Conant, W. Church. "John Ericsson, The Engineer." *Scribner's Magazine,* VII (January-June 1890).

[123] Sleeman, 331, and Grant, Ellsworth S., *The Colt Legacy: The Colt Armory in Hartford 1885-1980* (Providence, Rhode Island: Mowbray Company, 1982), 1-6. The latter was first published as "Gun Maker to the World," *American Heritage,* XIX (June 1968), 86-91.

[124] Sleeman, 331.

[125] Barnes, John Sanford. *Submarine Warfare, Offensive and Defensive: Including a Discussion of the Offensive Torpedo System, Its Effects Upon Iron-clad Ship Systems, and Influence Upon Future Naval Wars.* New York: Van Nostrand, 1969, 91.

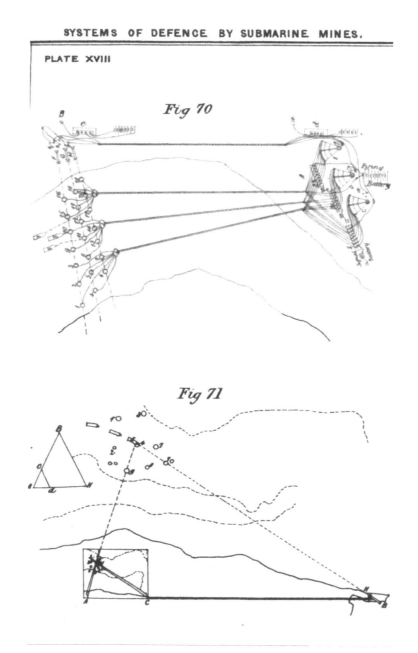

Figure 11. This was Colt's plan for a minefield with two operators who could locate the exact spot when a ship was over a "Torpedo." His mine fields were to contain 16 to 29 mines. (U.S. Government Printing Office)

Date	Craft, Name, Event or Country	Event, Builder and Boat Specifications	City, River, Lake, Sea, Ocean
1842[126]	Col. Samuel Colt Electric Submarine Torpedo	Colt had made several improvements of insulated copper wire, wet-cell batteries, and triggering mechanisms. He sank the target ship five miles away.	New York, U.S.A.
1842[127]	July 4 Col. Samuel Colt Electric Submarine Torpedo	This time his mine operator was on board another U.S. Navy man-of-war a great distance from the target ship when he sank it.	Castle Gardens, New York
1842[128]	August 20 Col. Samuel Colt Electric Submarine Torpedo	Similar experiment of the submarine electric mine. The operator was five miles away when he exploded the mine sinking the ship.	Potomac River U.S.A.
1843[129]	April 20 Col. Samuel Colt Electric Submarine Torpedo	In this test, the target vessel was a 500-ton ship moving at five knots at a distance of five miles. The crew on the trial ship left just before the time for the torpedo exploded.	New York, U.S.A.

Figure 12. Samuel Colt was a leader in the industry of "Electric-Torpedo Warfare." (Library of Congress).

---

[126] Sleeman, 332, and Grant, 1–6.
[127] Sleeman, 332, and Grant, 1–6.
[128] *Ibid.*
[129] *Ibid.*

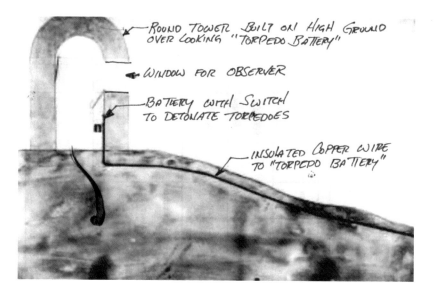

Figure 13. This "Torpedo Tower" was the heart of Colt's submarine mine field. He planned for 100' towers to be built, each with trigger mechanisms to operate the galvanic batteries. The operator was expected to sit in a cold tower for months on end, waiting foran enemy ship to park itself over the "Torpedo Barrage Field." Original art by Samuel Colt, annotations by the author. (U.S.Government Printing Office)

Figure 14.*The Last Experiment of Mr. Colt's Submarine Battery.* This painting was done by A. Gilbert. It is doubtful that Gilbert attended the demonstration. He was supplied sketches declared by Colt to be factually "correct." (U.S. Government Printing Office)

Date	Craft, Name, Event or Country	Event, Builder and Boat Specifications	City, River, Lake, Sea, Ocean
1844[130]	Capt. Warner "Invisible Shell"	On July 20, Captain Warner destroyed the ship *John o'Gaunt* with an underwater-device. He marketed his invention as an "invisible shell," but a subsequent Parliamentary investigation revealed that "the destruction of the *John o'Gaunt* was a trick of the same class as the blowing up of the punt on the fish-pond, which consisted merely of shells sunk and anchored under the water, and a long rope attached to the punt, which at a signal given was drawn by a team of horses, and which on striking the composition blew up the vessel. The destruction of the *John o'Gaunt* was just the same, except that a steamer was employed to drag the vessel to unavoidable destruction instead of a team of horses."[131][132]	Brighton, England
1845[133]	January 1 Col. Samuel Colt Electric Submarine Torpedo	The last and best testing of the "Electric Submarine Torpedo" against a target ship 40 miles distance from the operator.	New York, U.S.A.
1846[134]	Professor Schonbein Gun-Cotton	The professor was the inventor of an explosive that would have a profound effect on the world. By 1863, Professor Abel had brought this form of explosive up to standards for military use.	New York, U.S.A.
1846[135]	Sobrcro Nitro-Glycerin	This discovery was intended for blasting purposes. It would become a deadly agent in warfare in the hands of M. Alfred Nobel in 1863.	New York, U.S.A.

---

[130] Sleeman, 332.

[131] *HC Deb 25 June 1847 vol 93 cc921-46* http://hansard.millbanksystems.com/commons/1847/jun/25/captain-warners-inventions#S3V0093P0-01185

[132] See also Burke, Edmund (ed.) *Annual Register, or a view of the History and Politics of the Year 1844* (London: Longwood and Company, 1845) for a vivid description of the mysterious explosion.

[133] Sleeman, 332, and Grant, 1–6.

[134] Sleeman, 332.

[135] *Ibid.*

Date	Craft, Name, Event or Country	Event, Builder and Boat Specifications	City, River, Lake, Sea, Ocean
1854[136]	Russian Navy Stationary Submarine Mine	This is the first military use of stationary submarine "mines" (torpedoes). The Russians were able to place several mines near the English men-of-war *HMS Merlin* and *HMS Firefly*. The only effect noticed after detonation was the crew was wet.	Kronsdtadt Harbor St. Petersburg
1856[137]	John Ericcson Sub-Aquatic Torpedo Gun	A young Ericcson spent years working out the theories for the armored battle ship and underwater artillery. He approached the Emperor Napoleon III with designs for an armored, turreted battleship and his sub-aquatic "Torpedo Gun". Ericcson and his concepts impressed the Emperor, but the Emperor never contacted Ericcson again.	France
1860[138]	U.S.Navy Brutus DeVilleroi *USS Alligator*	DeVilleroi began building working submarines in the 1830's.His success in France prompted him to move to America. He built a test model, 35' long, for demonstration to the U.S. Navy. The design was accepted and he immediately began work on a full size submarine.	Delaware River Philadelphia

Figure 15. The *Alligator* was never in the category of a "Diving Boat" or "Semi-Submersible." It was a true submarine in that the crew could breathe and work with clean oxygen generated by chemicals carried on board the vessel. (Illustration by author).

---

[136] *Ibid.*

[137] Banard, Charles. "Ericsson's *Destroyer* and Her New Gun." *Scribner's Monthly Magazine*, 21 (March 1881, No. 5), 689-693.

[138] Maloney, Janet M. "Portrait of Possibility: The Submarine Alligator." *Civil War Times*, XLIV (No. 5, December, 2005), 34-40 and Bolander, L.H. The *Alligator, First Federal Submarine of the Civil War* (Annapolis: Naval Institute Press, June 1938).

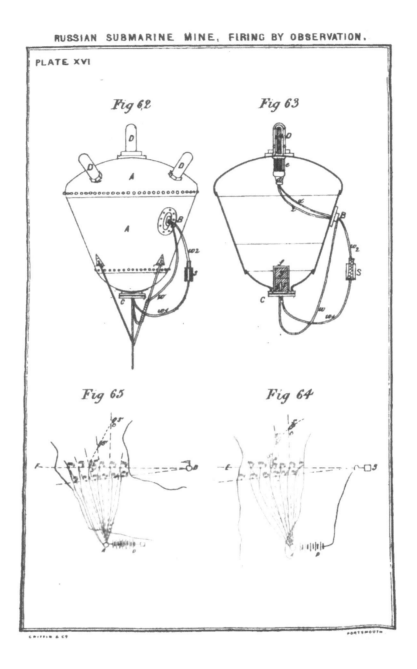

Figure 16. Russian stationary submarine mines. Russian was the first country in the world to embrace torpedo and mine warfare as a part of a country's naval doctrine. (Sleeman)

Date	Craft, Name, Event or Country	Event, Builder and Boat Specifications	City, River, Lake, Sea, Ocean
1861[139]	April USS Pawnee	The *USS Pawnee* saved the *USS Cumberland* from capture by Confederate forces in Norfolk, Virginia. The *Pawnee* received the surrender of Alexandria, Virginia on May 24, 1865, by a ship's boarding party. Confederate sources claim sinking the *Pawnee*. Claim disputed!	Atlantic Ocean
1861[140]	July 31 USS Richmond	This ship, captured by the U.S. Navy from the Confederates, fought in almost every major engagement of the Civil War. Confederates reported her sunk by torpedoes. Claim disputed!	Atlantic Ocean
1862[141]	February 14 USS Susquehanna	A launch from the *USS Susquehanna*, a side-wheel frigate, struck a submarine torpedo and received slight damage.	Wright River Georgia
1862[142]	February 18 Confederates Submarine Torpedoes	U.S. Navy gunboats attempting to force their way up the Savannah River were delayed by stationary submarine torpedoes laid by the Confederates. The fleet sustained no damage but naval warfare had turned a corner. The American navy was now on the defensive.	Savannah River, Georgia
1862[143]	December 12 USS Cairo	The ironclad *USS Cairo* ran over two large Confederate stationary submarine torpedoes. The explosions shattered most of the ship and it sank in 12 minutes with a great loss of life, off Haines Bluff, Mississippi.	Yazoo River Expedition

---

[139] Dictionary of American Naval Fighting Ships, V, 239.

[140] DANFS, VI, 102-103.

[141] Infernal-Machines.com. "Civil War Torpedoes, Ships Sunk or Damaged by Civil War Torpedoes," http://www.infernal-machines.com.

[142] Sleeman, 333.

[143] Sleeman, 333, and DANFS, II, 9.

Figure 17. The *Pawnee* was in almost every single action of importance during the times of the protracted war. She was claimed sunk several times by the Confederates and obviously, they were wrong about this also. (Library of Congress Prints and Photographs Division).

Figure 18. The capture of the *Richmond* so early in the war became an embarrassment to the citizens of Richmond, Virginia, who considered their city to be "sacred." (Library Of Congress Prints and Photographs Division)

Figure 19. This sketch shows the fanciful flights of fancy that people took in regards to the new technology. The artist shows the *Winona* completely submerged which was impossible. The David Class torpedo boat was a semi-submersible but not a submarine. Notice that on the bow the artist drew in the dive planes that were used on later models of the *David*. (Library of Congress Prints and Photographs Division)

Figure 20.The *USS Cairo* was the first craft of the Civil War to be sunk by a submarine torpedo. (Library of Congress)

Date	Craft, Name, Event or Country	Event, Builder and Boat Specifications	City, River, Lake, Sea, Ocean
1863[144]	January 1 USS Kinsman (ex-Gray Cloud)	Built as the side-wheel steamships *SS Grey Cloud,* the ship was seized in New Orleans and fitted out as a U. S. Army gunboat. The ship became damaged in a firefight with the *CSS Cotton* (ironclad gunboat) and ran over a contact submarine torpedo mear Franklin, Louisiana, in the Bayou Teche. The explosion unshipped the rudder. The ship did sink in Berwick Bay, Brasher City, Louisiana, on February 23, 1863. Six men died in the explosion.	Franklin, Alabama, Bayou Teche
1863[145]	January 8 Julia Hamilton	The English sloop was working as a blockade runner when she was captured by the U.S. Navy. The ship was sold to the American navy as a tender for the Northern Blockading Squadron. The Confederates reported her sunk by torpedoes. The claim cannot be confirmed.	Atlantic Ocean
1863[146]	February 28 USS Montauk	The *USS Montauk,* monitor type, destroyed the blockade-runner *CSN Rattlesnake* in the Ogeechee River. The boat then made contact with a submarine stationary torpedo and sustained damage. By April 1, 1863, the *Montauk* was part of the fleet that attacked Charleston.	Ogeechee River, Georgia
1863[147]	April 7 USS Weehawken	The single turreted monitor ship put up quite a fight in Charleston Harbor. The ship received 53 hits from Confederate shore batteries. As the ship withdrew to calmer waters, it struck a stationary submarine torpedo. The torpedo exploded directly under the ships heavy keel and caused no damage.	Charleston Harbor Charleston, S.C.
1863[148]	July 13 USS Baron de Kalb (ex-Saint Louis)	The USN stern-wheel ironclad gunboat, *USS Baron de Kalb* (originally *USS Saint Louis*) sank after running over two stationary mines near Yazoo City, Mississippi.	Yazoo River

[144] Infernal-Machines.com. "Civil War Torpedoes, Ships Sunk or Damaged by Civil War Torpedoes" www.infernal-machines.com . U.S. Naval Historical Center. "USS Ships-USS Kinsman (1863-1863)." http://www.history.navy.mil/photos/sh-usn-usnsh-k/kinsman. DANFS, III, 655-656.
[145] DANFS, 573.
[146] Sleeman, 333.
[147]Sleeman, 333, and DANFS VIII, 190-191.
[148] Sleeman, 333, and DANFS I, 98.

Figure 21. The only damage done to the *Kinsman* from striking a submarine torpedo was that the ships rudder was unshipped. The repairs were effected in a few hours and she was back in battle form. (Library of Congress Prints and Photographs Division).

Figure 22. The *USS Weehawken* is pushing a torpedo clearing raft on its bow. This "anti-torpedo device" did work amazingly well. It carried several drag chins suspended around the edges of the raft to detonate the submerged "Torpedoes." This was another invention of John Ericsson. (Library Of Congress Prints and Photographs Division)

Date	Craft, Name, Event or Country	Event, Builder and Boat Specifications	City, River, Lake, Sea, Ocean
1863[149]	August 8 *USS Commodore Barney*	The *USS Commodore Barney*, gunboat, sank after hitting a stationary submarine torpedo. The Confederates had placed a submarine torpedo with 1,750 pounds of black-powder fired by an on-shore electrical battery. The ship became damaged and 20 members of the crew died. The engine no longer functioned and the ship was towed for the rest of its tour in the area. The ship was fully repaired and returned to service, April 13, 1864.	James River Virginia
1863[150]	August 21 *CSS Torch*	The *Torch* was a unique design. It was a screw-propelled steamer with a triple-spar arrangement. The boat carried six spar charges, each weighing 75 pounds. Her attack on the *USS New Ironsides* failed for an unknown reason.	Charleston Harbor
1863[151]	September *USN John Farrow*	The U.S. transport *John Farrow* ran over a submarine torpedo and sustained serious damage.	Charleston Harbor
1863[152]	October 5 Confederate Navy Spar-Torpedo Boat I	This was the first use of a Spar-Torpedo boat built and used by any military force. The *CSS David* was built to sink the giant ironclad, *USS New Ironsides,* in Charleston Harbor. The attack was successful. The sixty-pound charge at the tip of the spar caused enough damage to keep the *New Ironsides* out of action the rest of the war.	Charleston Harbor
1863[153]	Confederate Navy *CSS Marion, Ettiwa*	The Confederate Navy lost two ships, *CSS Marion* and *CSS Ettiwa,* to their own submarine torpedoes while laying mines intended for American navy ships.	Charleston Harbor
1863[154]	Confederate Navy *Squib*-class Torpedo Boat *CSS Shultz*	The Confederate used the Squib class spar-torpedo boat as a courier boat referred to as a "Flag of Truce Boat." The *CSS Shultz,* when returning to Richmond after a prisoner of war exchange, blew up in an explosion from a Confederate torpedo.	James River Virginia

---

[149] Sleeman, 333 and DANFS II, 153-154.

[150] DANFS II, Confederate Naval Vessels, 364.

[151] Sleeman, 333.

[152] Sleeman, 333 and DANFS, Confederate Forces, II, 513-514.

[153] Sleeman, 333 and DANFS, Confederate Forces, VII, 518, 547

Figure 23. Illustration of the *USS Commodore Barney* striking a Confederate torpedo. (Library Of Congress Prints and Photographs Division)

---

[154] Smart, Larry R. "Evolution of the Torpedo Boat," *Military Affairs*, 23 (No. 2, Summer, 1959) 97-101. DANFS, Confederate Forces, II, 565.,

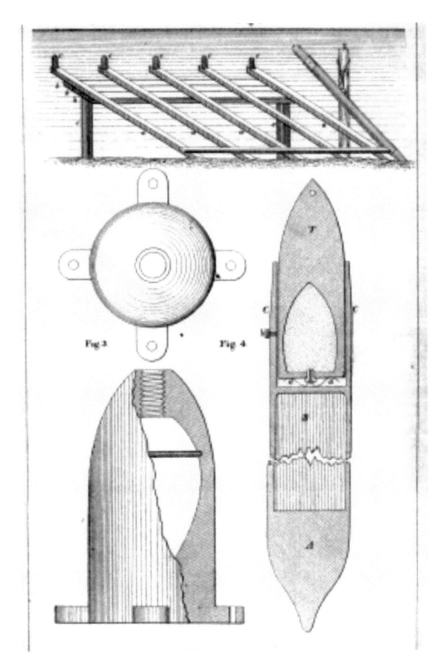

Figure 24. The Confederate Torpedo Department perfected the frame torpedo and they proved to be deadly. (Sleeman, 40)

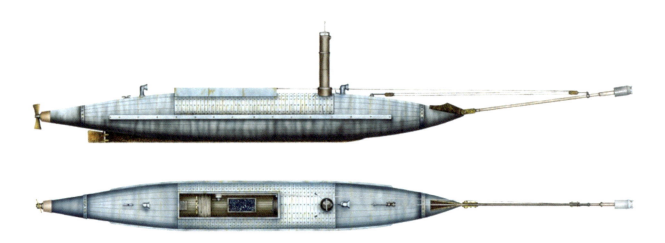

Figure 25. The *CSS David* was the first purpose-built spar-torpedo boat built by any Government. It was a direct design taken from the only spar-torpedo boat design in the world of Robert Fulton of 1830. (Illustration by author).

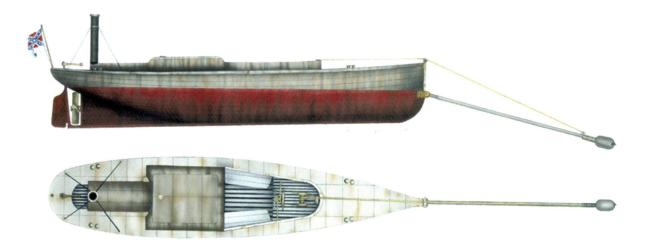

Figure 26. The craft was well built but manned by any one of any real competence. The boat became know and used for "Flag of Truce" boat or a "Surrender Boat". None of this design ever sank an enemy vessel. (Illustration by author)

Figure 27. *USS Housatonic* under attack. (Library of Congress Prints and Photographs Division)

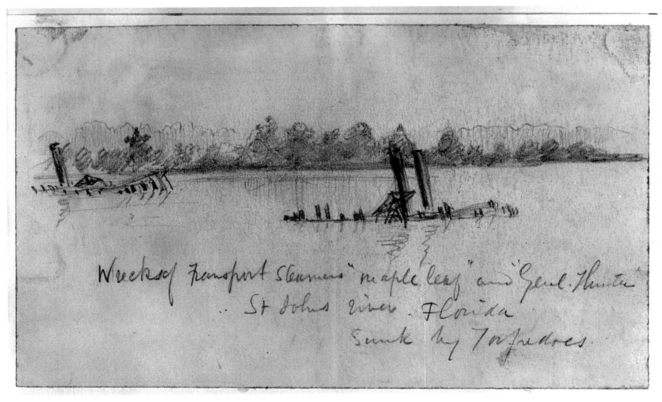

Figure 28. The *USS Maple Leaf* and *General Hunter* fell victim to two or more large 'Submarine Torpedoes' planted by members of the Confederate Torpedo Department. (Library Of Congress Prints and Photographs Division)

Date	Craft, Name, Event or Country	Event, Builder and Boat Specifications	City, River, Lake, Sea, Ocean
1864[155]	February 8 USS Rose (ex-Ai Fitch)	The screw tug was operating in New York Harbor when obtained by the U. S. Navy. They fitted her with one 20-pounder Parrot rifle and one 12-pounder gun. The Confederates reported her sunk. No confirmation.	Atlantic Ocean
1864[156]	February 17 USS Housatonic	The H. L. Hunley sank the USS Housatonic, and herself, after striking the ship with a spar torpedo. This would be the first spar-torpedo vessel to sink a capital ship. The Hunley sank due to faulty design and construction.	Charleston Harbor
1864[157]	February Spar-Torpedo Boat CSS Midge	The Midge was made along the lines of the CSS David in Charleston, South Carolina. US Army forces captured the Midge in February and moved the boat to New York Navy Yard for display.	Charleston, South Carolina
1864[158]	March 6 USS Memphis	The Memphis, built in Scotland for the Confederate Navy, and captured by the USS Magnolia and the U. S. Navy purchased her from the Prize Court and placed into service, September 4, 1862. A Squib class spar torpedo boat attempted to sink the USS Memphis in the North Edisto River. The spar mounted torpedoes malfunctioned and the Memphis suffered no damage.	North Edisto River South Carolina
1864[159]	April 1 Maple Leaf	The Confederates, using floating torpedoes, sank the Maple Leaf, a transport ship.	St. John's River Florida
1864[160]	April 15 USS Eastport	During the early stages of the Red River Expedition the ship was damaged by a Confederate torpedo and run aground. The damage was beyond repair and destroyed to prevent capture.	Grand Ecore

---

[155] DANFS, II, 518

[156] Sleeman, 333, and DANFS, III, 370-371f

[157] Confederate Ships-Midge (1864-1865) http://history.navy.mil/photos/sh-us-cs/csa-sh.csash-mr/midge.htm; Ships Sunk or Damaged by Civil War Torpedoes <http://www.infernal –machines.com/_sgg/f10245.htm> and DANFS, II, 548-549.

[158] Sleeman, 333, and DANFS, IV, 317-318.

[159] Sleeman, 333, and "Ships Sunk or Damaged by Civil War Torpedoes" <http://www.infernal-machines.com/_sgg/f10245>.

[160] DANFS, II, 32.

Date	Craft, Name, Event or Country	Event, Builder and Boat Specifications	City, River, Lake, Sea, Ocean
1864[161]	April 9 *USS Minnesota*	The *Squib* made a night attack and damaged the *USS Minnesota* without sinking her. Most *Squib* pilots lacked training to cause real damage to U.S. Navy ships.	Newport News, Hampton Roads
1864[162]	April 18 *USS Wabash*	A *Squib* class spar torpedo boat made an attack on the *USS Wabash*, a naval frigate, and the attempt failed. The pilot showed lack of training by the Confederate Navy Spar-Torpedo Boat Department.	Charleston Harbor
1864[163]	May 6 *USS H.A. Weed*	The U.S. transport, *USS H.A. Weed*, sank after detonating a submarine mine.	St. Johns River
1864[164]	May *CSS St. Patrick*	The small *David* class spar-torpedo boat, built by John P. Hailigan, Mobile Alabama, failed to inflict any damage on the USS *Octorara* in Mobile Bay. The mission was aborted when her boiler burst, killing one man and causing serious injury to another.	Mobile Bay, AL
1864[165]	June 19 *USS Alice Wood*	The U.S. transport, *USS Alice Wood,* is destroyed by a submarine mine.	St. Johns River
1864[166]	August 5 *USS Tecumseh*	The monitor class *USS Tecumseh sank* from a submarine torpedo while attacking the defenses of Mobile Bay. The explosion was large enough to cause the ship to immediately role and "turn turtle'. It sank in 25 seconds with 93 men including its very courageous captain, Commander T.A.M. Craven.	Mobile Bay, AL

---

[161] DANFS, Confederate Forces, II, 567.

[162] Sleeman, 334, and DANFS, VIII, 5-7.

[163] Sleeman, 334.

[164] Smart, Larry R. "Evolution of the Torpedo Boat" *Military Affairs,* 23, No. 2, Summer, 1959, 97-101; DANFS, Confederate Forces, II, 567.

[165] Sleeman, 334.

[166] Sleeman, 334, and DANFS, VII, 78.

Figure 29. The fear of Torpedoes became a major concern for the ships commanders. Morale dropped to new lows after the introduction of the stationary and floating torpedo. (U.S. Government Printing Office)

Figure 30. While Matthew Fontaine Maury was an officer in the U.S. Navy, he met with Samuel Colt on several occasions. He became interested in Colt's "Submarine Batter" and knew first hand of all of Colt's many accomplishments. It was Maury who established the Confederate Torpedo Department early in the war. Maury is also famous as a pioneer in oceanography. (U.S. Government Printing Office)

NIMBLE BOOKS LLC

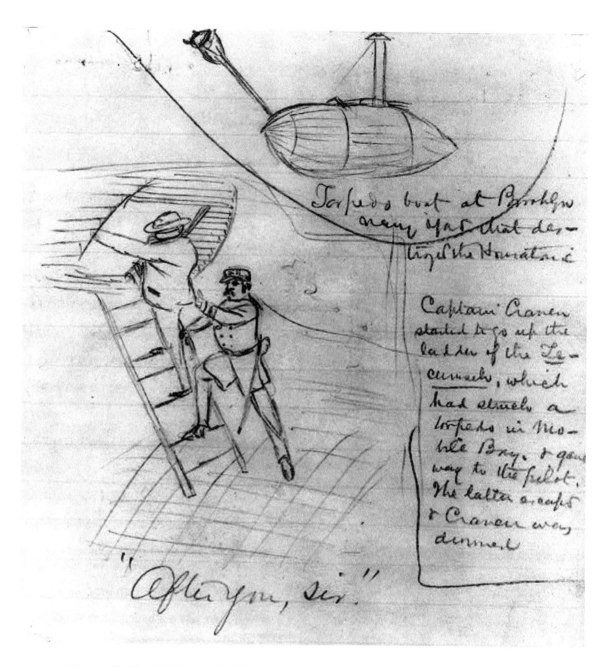

Figure 31. The *USS Craven* had been attacked by a *David* Class spar-torpedo boat. While the vessel was sinking Captain T.A.M. Craven died while assisting his men out of the ship. (Library of Congress Prints and Photographs Division)

84

Date	Craft, Name, Event or Country	Event, Builder and Boat Specifications	City, River, Lake, Sea, Ocean
1864[167]	September 9 *CSS Squib*	Built in Richmond, Virginia, at Tredegar Ironworks, the *Squib* quickly became a class of spar torpedo boat. Small and agile, it is the best spar torpedo boat of the Civil War. The Squib moved in to Hampton Roads to attack the frigate, *USS Minnesota* with a single spar-torpedo with a 53 pound charge. The attack failed causing next to no damage to the ship. It is believed that she was sunk or captured in the final days of the Civil War in the Battle for Trent's Reach, James River.	Hampton Roads, VA
1864[168]	October 27 USN Picket Boat No. 1	This is only successful attack by a spar-torpedo boat of the Civil War. The converted Picket Boat came armed with a Wood Lay torpedo of a greatly advanced design. Lt. Cushing and his small crew accepted the assignment to attack the *CSS Albemarle*, the South's newest and most powerful ironclad. The Albemarle's destruction was complete.	Roanoke River Plymouth, N.C.
1864[169]	November 27 *Greyhound*	The *USS Greyhound,* a transport ship, suffered its loss by the act of a Confederate saboteur. Confederates were supplied with "Coal Torpedoes". These explosive looked like lumps of coal and were easily placed in the coal bunkers on U.S.Navy ships.	James River. VA
1864[170]	December 12 *USS Narcissus* (ex-Mary Cook)	Like many other gun boats the *Narcissus* performed as a minesweeper in Mobile Bay. Caught in a severe storm off Mobile the ship struck a floating torpedo and sank in 15 minutes. There was no loss of life. The ship was raised and put back into action	Mobile Bay, AL
1864[171]	December 9 *USS Otsego, USS Bazeby*	The American steamers *USS Otsego* and *USS Bazeby* were destroyed with a great loss of life by Confederate submarine torpedoes. The Otsego struck first and the Bazeby, while coming to her aid, struck the other mine.	Roanoke River

---

[167] DANFS II, 567.
[168] *Official Records of the Union and Confederate Navies in the War of the Rebellion*. "Torpedo used by Lieutenant Cushing in the destruction of the Confederate States Ram Albemarle,"Series I, Volume 10, 1900, 623.
[169] Sleeman, 334.
[170] Sleeman, 334, and DANFS V, 11-12.
[171] Civil War Torpedoes, Ships Sunk or Damaged by Civil War Torpedoes <http://www.infernal-machines>, Accessed by author November 24,2007; Sleeman, 334

LIEUT. CUSHING'S TORPEDO BOAT SINKING THE ALBEMARLE ON ROANOKE RIVER, N. C.

Figure 32. This is the only spar-torpedo boat of the Civil War to actually and fully sink an enemy ship. Lt. John Cushing took the well designed, boat and torpedo, by Engineer William W. Wood, and sank the newest and most heavily armed Ironclad of the South. (U.S. Navy Historical Department)

Figure 33. Lieutenant William B. Cushing planned and executed a daring and daunting mission to attack and sink the newest, most powerful ironclad, in the Confederate fleet. He lost a good number of men captured or killed in the attack. (U.S. Navy Historical Department)

Figure 34. This U.S. Army officer is setting up the Haupt's torpedo for destroying a bridge. After the many successes of the Confederate Torpedo Department, the U.S. services followed suit. (Library Of Congress Prints and Photographs Division)

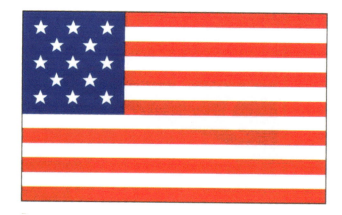

Figure 35. U.S. Navy "Boat Flag" 1862. (U.S. Government Printing Office)

Date	Craft, Name, Event or Country	Event, Builder and Boat Specifications	City, River, Lake, Sea, Ocean
1864[172]	M.A. Nobel "Dynamite"	Nobel was able to make the raw Nitroglycerine into a safer yet powerful explosive form, Dynamite.	U.S.A.
1864[173]	Captain Lupuis & Mr. Whitehead	The Captain asked Mr. Whitehead for assistance in developing his "Automobile Torpedo Boat." Whitehead's interest in the Captain's problem led to the full operational modern torpedo.	Fiume, Austria
1865[174]	January 15 USS Patapsco	While covering picket boats dragging for submarine torpedoes the monitor ironclad USS Patapsco stuck and detonated a submarine torpedo, deep under her keel The ship sank in less than one minute. Sixty-two men went down with the ship.	Charleston Harbor, S. C.
1865[175]	January 20 USS Osceola	The USS Osceola, a side-wheel, double-ended gunboat, became crippled after striking a Confederate drifting torpedo. Not verified.	Cape Fear River, N. C.
1865[176]	January 25 US Navy Spuyten Duyvil	The USN Torpedo Boat No.5 Spuyten Duyvil successfully launched two Wood Lay torpedoes in a test off Mystic, Connecticut. Chief Engineer William W.W. Wood and 1st Assistant Engineer, John L. Lay designed this and five other craft.	New Haven, Conn. Atlantic Ocean
1865[177]	January 23 Spuyten Duyvil	For the first time since her arrival, the spar-torpedo boat was ordered into position to support the twin-turreted monitor class warship, U.S.S. Onondaga. This was a serious misuse of the craft. The Onondaga would have been better served if the Spuyten Duyvil had attacked the Confederate Navy's James River Fleet.	Trent's Reach James River

---

[172] Sleeman, 334.

[173] Gray, Edwyn. *The Devil's Device: Robert Whitehead and the History of the Torpedo* at 34. London: Seeley, Service & Co., 1991.

[174] Sleeman, 335, and DANFS, V, 224-225.

[175] Sleeman, 335, and DANFS, V, 180.

[176] *Official Records of the Union and Confederate Navies in the War of the Rebellion*. Report of Assistant Engineer, John L. Lay, U.S.N, Commander, USN Torpedo Boat No.5, *Spuyten Duyvil*.

[177] Official Records of the Union and Confederate Navies in the War of the Rebellion: Report of Assistant Engineer, John L. Lay, U.S.N, Commander,   USN Torpedo Boat No.5, *Spuyten Duyvil*.

Figure 36. U.S. Navy Commodore's Broad Pennant. (U.S. Navy Historical Department)

Figure 37. Hand drawn illustrations such as this one of *USS Patapsco* were the early equivalent of camera. Unfortunately, most bear no signature or date.

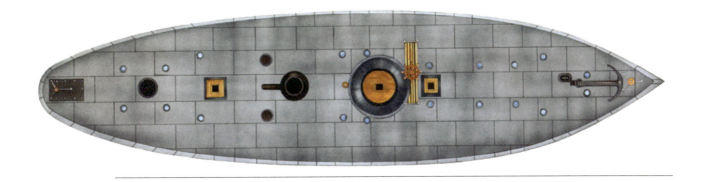

Figure 38. The U.S. Navy *Torpedo Boat No. 5, Spuyten Duyvil* was a most successful feat of engineering since the USS *Monitor*. It came out of the yards working perfectly. (Illustrations by author)

Date	Craft, Name, Event or Country	Event, Builder and Boat Specifications	City, River, Lake, Sea, Ocean
1865[178]	January 23/24 CSS Wasp	The *Wasp* was one of four spar torpedo boats attached to the Confederate James River Fleet. The boat's crew attempted to remove obstructions laid by earlier Confederate forces That had made the break-out of the fleet an impossibility.	Trent's Reach James River
1865[179]	January 23/24 CSS Hornet	During the attempted breakout of the Confederate James River Fleet, the *Hornet* collided with the much larger ship, *C.S. Allison* in Trent's Reach.	Trent's Reach James River
1865[180]	January 23/24 CSS Torpedo	The *Torpedo* was a tender for the spar-torpedo boat flotilla. The ship was 70' long and at 150 tons substantial in a fight with her twp 20-pounder guns. The ship failed to make it out of the Trent's Reach entanglements.	Trent's Reach James River
1865[181]	January 28 CSS Saint Patrick	The *St. Patrick* attacked the *USS Octorara* in Mobile Bay of January 28. The spar torpedo misfired and the *Octorara* sustained no damage.	Mobile Bay Mobile, AL
1865[182]	February CSS Midge	The *Midge* was similar in design to the *David*. It was built in Charleston, South Carolina, in 1864. The *Midge* was captured by U. A. Army forces in February 1865. The boat was taken to the New York Navy Yard and put on exhibit until 1877. The boat's fate is then unknown.	Charleston Harbor Charleston,S.C.
1865[183]	March 1 USS Harvest Moon	This was the flagship of Admiral John A. Dalhgren; *USS Harvest Moon* sank from a submarine torpedo in an area just swept for torpedoes.	Winyan Bay Georgetown
1865[184]	March 4 USS Thorne	The U.S.Navy transport *USS Thorne* hit a stationary submarine torpedo and sank in the Cape Fear River.	Cape Fear River

---

[178] DANFS, Confederate Naval Vessels, II, 367.

[179] *Ibid.*

[180] *Ibid.*

[181] Torpedo Boats < http://www.infernal-machine.com/_sgg/f10235.htm> Accessed by Author November, 2005; DANFS, VII, 503

[182] Confederate Ships-Midge (1864-1865) <http://www.history.navy.mil/photos/sh-us-cs/csa-sh/csah-mr/midge.htm> Accessed By Author, 2006

[183] Sleeman, 334 and DANFS III, 259

[184] Sleeman, 334.

Figure 39. This is a portrait of the Confederate submarine sent out to sink the *USS Minnesota,* a U.S. Navy ship of the line. Like most Confederate efforts to use "Diving-Boats" to destroy U.S. Navy ships, the mission was a dismal failure. (Library of Congress Prints and Photographs Division)

Figure 40. This illustration, by an unknown solider or sailor, paints the grimy picture that "Torpedoes" were to the men who manned the ships on the river fleets, completely terrifying. These barrel torpedoes could seldom be seen in time and when in groups of three or more could be quite deadly. (Library of Congress Prints and Photographs)

Date	Craft, Name, Event or Country	Event, Builder and Boat Specifications	City, River, Lake, Sea, Ocean
1865[185]	March 12 USS Althea	The screw-tug Althea (originally Alfred A. Wotkyns) had been assigned to the Northern Blockading Squadron and then ship later assigned to the James River Squadron. Here the boat was used as a tug, tender and spar-torpedo boat. A stationary submarine torpedo sank the ship on March 12th. The boat was raised later and stayed in service until 1866.	Blakely River
1865[186]	March 12 USS Jonquil	The USS Jonquil (originally J.K. Kirkman) joined in with others clearing submarine torpedoes in Charleston Harbor. Crewmembers were in the process of de-fusing the torpedo when it exploded. Three men were wounded and nine knocked in to water. The minor repairs were completed by the next morning and the ship was back to work, clearing torpedoes.	Charleston Harbor Charleston, S.C.
1865[187]	March 28 USS Milwaukee	The U.S. Navy monitor class USS Milwaukee hit a stationary submarine torpedo and sank.	Blakely River
1865[188]	March 29 USS Osage	The U.S. Navy monitor class, USS Osage struck a drifting torpedo and sank.	Blakely River
1865[189]	April 1 USS Rodolph Gun-Boat No. 48	The side-wheeler, gun-boat, tin clad, USS Rodolph, No.48, had been one of the most combative boats in the US Navy. The boat served its last year as a "Mine Sweeper.". While towing a barge with salvage equipment, it struck a submarine torpedo and sank. 4 crewmen died and 11 were wounded.	Blakely River

---

[185] Sleeman, 335, and DANFS I, 38.
[186] Sleeman, 335, and DANFS VII, 559.
[187] Sleeman, 335, and DANFS, IV, 362.
[188] Sleeman, 335, and DANFS, V, 565.
[189] Sleeman, 335, and DANFS , VI, 147.

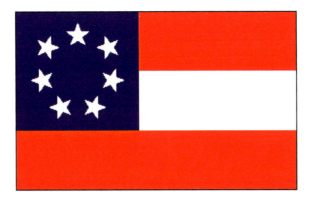

Figure 41. The Confederate States of America went through several versions of a national standard. It turns out there was no unity in ever selecting a design. Every Confederate state wanted their own flag. Up into the closing days of the war, Southern politicians still argued about the flag. (U.S. Government Printing Office)

Figure 42. The South used a large number of "Flag of Truce Vessels." (Library of Congress)

Date	Craft, Name, Event or Country	Event, Builder and Boat Specifications	City, River, Lake, Sea, Ocean
1865[190]	April 3 CSS Wasp, Hornet, Scorpion	The *Squib* class *CSS Wasp* helped to refloat the spar-torpedo boat *CSS Hornet* in the James River. Later the boat tried to tow the *CSS Scorpion* off shore where she had run aground and the *Wasp* became grounded in the attempt. The *Scorpion* was abandoned and captured by U.S. Navy forces.	Trent's Reach James River
1865[191]	April 13 USS Ida Gun Boat	The U.S.Navy gunboat *USS Ida* struck a stationary submarine torpedo. The boilers burst, timbers on the starboard side were crushed in, the deck turned into a mass of splinters. Three crewmembers wounded and two died.	Mobile Bay Mobile, AL
1865[192]	April 14 USS *Scotia* Gun Boat	The "90-Day" gunboat *Scotia* built by Jacob Birley, J.P. Morris & Company, Philadelphia, 1862. Struck a submarine torpedo off Mobile and sank with a great loss of life.	Mobile Bay Mobile, Al
1865[193]	May 12 USS *R.B. Hamilton*	The U.S.Navy transport *R. B. Hamilton* hit a stationary submarine torpedo and sank.	Mobile Bay Mobile, AL
1865[194]	June 6 USS Jonquil Gun Boat	The crew of the gunboat *USS Jonquil* attempted to raise a set of 'Frame' torpedoes when the torpedoes accidentally detonated. The gunboat was destroyed with a great loss of life.	Ashley River
1866[195]	September 2 Paraguayan Navy	The Paraguayan Navy took notice of the success of "Torpedo Warfare" in the United States and adopted the technology. Their first use of stationary submarine torpedoes netted them the Brazilian war steamer *Rio Janeiro,* during a bombardment of the harbor and town.	Currupaity, Paraguay

---

[190] DANFS, Confederate Forces, II, 565.

[191] DANFS, III, 414-415.

[192] Sleeman, 335, and DANFS VI, 382-383.

[193] Sleeman, 335, and National Park Service, "Full Speed Ahead" <http://www.nps.gov/archive/vick/vistr/sitebltn/damntorp.htm>.

[194] Sleeman, 335, and DANFS III, 559.

[195]Sleeman, 335.

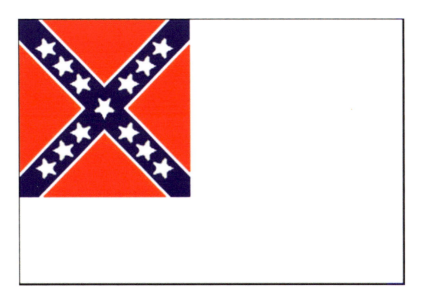

Figure 43. This rendition caused unmanageable problems for Confederate troops. When this largely white flag first appeared, it was commonly mistaken for a flag of surrender. Quickly, another flag was created with a broad red panel on its right side. (U.S. Government Printing Office)

Figure 44. The conspirators in the Lincoln assassination were kept handcuffed aboard the new ironclads. (U.S. Navy Historical Department)

Date	Craft, Name, Event or Country	Event, Builder and Boat Specifications	City, River, Lake, Sea, Ocean
1868[196]	Robert Whitehead "Fish Torpedo"	His first trials were highly successful and resulted in Austria being the first European nation to adopt the "Torpedo" doctrine.	Fiume Austria
1869[197]	Captain W. Harvey	Harvey favored perfecting the "towed" torpedo concept. His trials were never successful and his torpedo dropped from use.	Russia
1870[198]	John Ericsson Compressed Air Torpedo	His torpedo is all iron construction and steered by compressed air running through a flexible tube on a reel. From a shore installation or a ship, the device could be set up for use. Ericsson's torpedo tested by Commodore W.N. Jeffers, USN, received rave reviews for trouble-free performance and speed.	U.S.A.
1870[199]	German Navy	The Germans developed torpedo fleets, *Freiwillige Seewehr* (Voluntary Sea Force) using existing small boats fitted with torpedo equipment. They were to guard the Elbe and Weser estuaries.	Germany
1871[200]	England Rev. C. Ramus	Through his own inventiveness and dedicated research, the Reverend developed the concept for a "stepped" ship. This went with his patent for a planing boat without a "step." Models were made and tested of his concept boats that weighed in at 2,500 tons. His were the first ship models to be tested in indoor tanks.	England
1871[201]	British Navy *Miranda*	The *Miranda* was a lightly built steel boat with a speed of 16.4 knots. This is considered to be the precursor of the modern motor torpedo boat.	Great Britain

---

[196] Sleeman, 335, and Gray, Edwyn. *The Devil's Device: Robert Whitehead and the History of the Torpedo Service* (Seeley & Co. Ltd, 1991), 58-59.
[197] Sleeman, 335.
[198] Brown, Allen D. "Torpedoes and Torpedo Boats," *Harper's New Monthly Magazine*, LXV (June to November, 1882), 36-47
[199] Groner, Erich. *Die deutschen Kriegssniffe, 1815-1945* (J.F. Lehmanns Verlag Munchen, 1968).
[200] Fock, *Fast Fighting Boats*, 13.
[201] Fock, *Fast Fighting Boats*, 11.

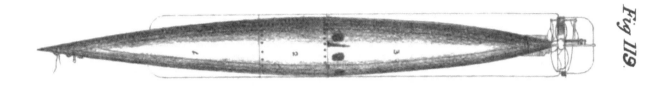

Figure 45. Robert Whitehead's first "Fish Torpedoes" were slow and erratic but they did lead to the ultimate stable design. (Sleeman, 226)

Figure 46. Ericsson created a clumsy but effective "Automobile Torpedo" which extended his reach into advanced technology. Later Brennan would create his wire-driven model based on this experiment. (U.S. Navy History Department)

Date	Craft, Name, Event or Country	Event, Builder and Boat Specifications	City, River, Lake, Sea, Ocean
1871[202]	German Navy *Devrient*	The boats, I-III, were modest performers. They functioned as defensive vessels in Wilhelmshaven Harbor, July 8, 1881.	Devrient, Danzig Germany
		Speed: 8.0 knots; **Displacement:** 24 tons; **Armament:** 1-Bow spar w/ 17kg. charge, w/impact fuse; **Length:** 20.3m; **Beam:** 3.30m; **Draft:** 1.9m; **Engines:** 1-250hp steam; Single Screw'	
1871[203]	German Navy *Waltjen*	Again, three boats built for spar experiments and later changed to minelayers for Wilhelmshaven Harbor. **Builder:** Waltjen & Co. **Speed:** 7.7 knots, **Displacement:** 24 tons, **Armament:** 1-Bow spar w/ 17kg charge, w/impact fuse; **Length:** 14.6m; **Beam:** 3.33m; **Draft:** 1.8m; **Engine:** 1-60hp steam; Single Screw.	Bremen, Germany
1873[204]	U.S. Navy 1st Asst Engineer John L. Lay	Lay introduced the Locomotive Controllable Torpedo. This was the beginning of "Wire-Guided" torpedo design for this era and the concept still used by the world's military arms manufacturers today.	U.S.A.
1873[205]	Royal Norwegian Navy *Wasp*	The Thorneycroft Company built its first spar-torpedo boat for Norway. **Speed:** 15 knots, Length: 57'	England
1874[206]	British Navy *Vesuvius*	An extremely strange design, but within keeping to the Victorian era of fantasy engineering and construction. The ship had no traditional funnel. Fumes exited via a long row of exhaust ducts along both sides of the rear deck. The boat burned only high-grade coke to prevent smoke. These features prefigured modern "stealth" designs.	England

---

[202] *Die deutschen Kriegssniffe, 1815-194*, I, 32.

[203] *Die deutschen Kriegssniffe, 1815-1945*, I, 32.

[204] Hughes, W. S. "Modern Aggressive Torpedo Boats." *Scribner's Magazine*, I (Issue 4, 1887), 427-437.

[205] Gray, 141. and *Historical Transaction 1893-1943*, 356.

[206] Personal communication with Gordon Smith, Naval-History.com, May 5 2008 and Gray, 142.

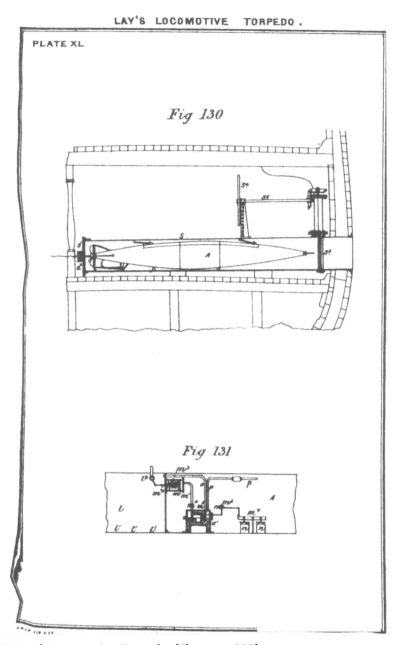

Figure 47. Lay's Locomotive Torpedo. (Sleeman, 232)

Date	Craft, Name, Event or Country	Event, Builder and Boat Specifications	City, River, Lake, Sea, Ocean
1874[207]	British Navy "Brennan Torpedo"	Irish born, Australian national, Louis P. Brennan, patents the device on February 1, 1878. Brennan invented the 'Wire-Driven Dirigible Torpedo". It used a steam engine to drive the winding engine with 18-gauge wire to control direction and speed. 1882. **Speed:** 20 knots; **Displacement:** 3.5 tons; **Length:** 24', **Diameter:** 24"; **Warhead:** 200 lbs. wet-guncotton; **Range:** 1.5 miles (2,640 yards)	England
1874[208]	U.S. Navy *Intrepid*	The Boston Navy Yard built a large, iron hulled, multiple spar torpedo boat backed up by heavy guns. Called a Steam Torpedo Ram, it was not a successful design.	U.S.A.
1875[209]	Royal Dutch Navy	The Yarrow company builds its first spar-torpedo boat for the Royal Dutch Navy. **Speed:** 17 knots	England
1876[210]	U.S. Navy *Lightning*	The Herreshoff brothers build their first highly successful spar-torpedo boat, Hull No.20. It was capable of going backward at the same speed as going forward by reversing engine and not using rudder. The boat could stop in its own length by reversing its engine. **Speed:** 17.5 knots; **Displacement :** Hull only, 2,800 lb; full weight, 6,900 lb; **Length:** 58'; B: 6'-3", **Draft:** (forward)-14", (Aft): 22"; **Engines:** Twin 5" Cyl. dia. x 10" stroke; **Armament:** 2-Steel spars 22' w/torpedoes w/ 301 lbs. dynamite; **Crew:** 2	U.S.A.

---

[207] Gray, 130-134.

[208] *Historical Transactions 1893-1943*, 356, and U.S. Navy Historical Center. "Intrepid." http://www.history.navy.mil/danfs/i2/intrepid-ii.htm

[209] *Historical Transactions 1893-1943*, 356

[210] Simpson, Richard V. *Building The Mosquito Fleet: The U. S. Navy's First Torpedo Boats*, (Arcadia Publishing, 2001). *Historical Transaction 1893-1943*, 356.

Figure 48. Australian Louis Brennan. carried forward Ericsson's idea of remote control of a torpedo through an early for of 'wire-guided' technology. Brennan Torpedo Stations were built in Europe and Asia. (Hong Kong Coastal Defense Museum)

MR. LOUIS P. BRENNAN, THE INVENTOR OF THE TORPEDO.

Figure 49. Louis Brennan.

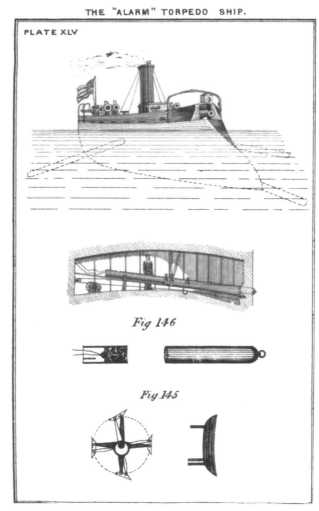

Figure 50. The *Alarm* was a very unsuccessful design. The "Old hands" in the U.S. Navy wanted to desperately hang on to the ram bow. This made the new torpedo boat virtually useless. (Sleeman, 274)

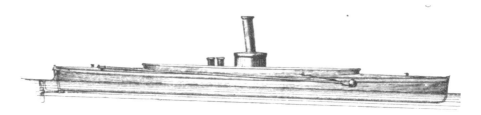

Figure 51.*USS Lightning* (Sleeman)

Date	Craft, Name, Event or Country	Event, Builder and Boat Specifications	City, River, Lake, Sea, Ocean
1876[211]	German Navy *Ziienten*	This is Germany's first purpose built torpedo boat. Designed for Whitehead torpedoes and no spars. The Thames Ironworks of England built it. The boat carried two underwater torpedo tubes, one aft, and one in the bow. The boat later carried 6-50mm (1.95") guns. **Speed:** 16 knots; **Displacement:** 1,152 tons; **Length:** 260'-6";B:28'; D:15'-2"; **Engines:** 2-Horizontal Compound steam; 2- screws, 2-Mast, 4-sails; **Armament:** 2-15" torpedo tubes, 6-50mm guns; **Crew:** 95	Germany
1877[212]	May 12 Russian Navy	The Russian launched a torpedo boat attack against several Turkish ships. The Russian were using towed torpedoes and a torpedo hit one Turkish ship, it failed to explode.	Batoum, Black Sea
1877[213]	May 27 Russian Navy *Shutka* and *Mina.*	Russian spar torpedo boats successfully attacked the Turkish ships *Fettu Islam, Duba Saife*, and *Kilidj Ali.* The monitor *Duba Saife* was sunk. Two of the Russian torpedo boats were made of iron, the *Shutka* and *Mina.*	Matchines River, Danube
1877[214]	May 29 *HMS Shah*	During the Battle of Pacocha, for the first time a warship fired a Whitehead 'Fish' torpedo against an enemy ship, the Peruvian Ironclad Huascar. The distance was too great and the torpedo ran out of fuel in the attempt.	Pacific Ocean

---

[211] Jackson, Robert. *Destroyers, Frigates, and Corvettes* (Barnes & Noble, Inc., 2000), 278.

[212] Greger, Rene "The Origins of Russian and Soviet MTBs" (*Warship*, IX, Issue 33), 38; Sleeman, 336.

[213] Sleeman, 336, and Greger, 38.

[214] Sleeman, 335; Memorials and Monuments in Plymouth City Centre (*HMS Shah*) www.memorials.inportsmouth.co.uk/city-centre/shah.htm ; The Huascar, http:/ members.lvcos.co.uk/Juan39.THE_HUASCAR.nm.

Figure 52. Russian Spar Torpedo Boats attacking a Turkish Man-of-War. (Richard Worth Collection)

Date	Craft, Name, Event or Country	Event, Builder and Boat Specifications	City, River, Lake, Sea, Ocean
1877[215]	June 9 Russian Navy *Torpedo Boat No.1* *(SK-1)*	The Russian torpedo boat commanders were reckless in pressing their attacks against the Turkish fleet. An attack of six wooden boats against the four heavily armed ironclads led to the lead boat, *Torpedo Boat No. 1* with her commander Lieutenant Poutschin and his crew were all taken prisoner. The other boats scattered.	Sulina, mouth of the Danube Black Sea
1877[216]	June 20 Russian Navy Spar Torpedo Boat *Choutka*	This action helped prove the foolhardiness of daytime attacks by spar torpedo boats. The single boat went after a Turkish monitor and the small boats commander became severely wounded from the larger ships gunfire. The wire to trigger the spar charge was cut by enemy fire and the attack failed.	Rutschuk, on the Danube Black Sea
1877[217]	June 23 Russian Navy Spar Torpedo Boats	Once again, the daylight tactics of the Russian boat commanders meant a doomed mission. Two boats set out to attack a Turkish monitor. The spirited defense of the Turks proved to be too much and the boats pulled back.	Mouth of the Aluta, Danube, Black Sea
1877[218]	August 22 Russian Navy Spar Torpedo Boats	The Turkish commander of the *Assari Shefket* adjusted to the Russian tactics by placing small guard boats out from his ship. When the four Russian boats moved to attack, they were driven off by heavy and relentless small arms fire.	Soukoum Kaleh, Black Sea
1877[219]	October 10 Russian Navy Electric Contact Mine	The Russians placed electric contact mines near the Turkish defenses of Sulina and sank a gunboat *Suna*. About fifteen officers and men were killed in the explosion	Sulina, Black Sea
1877[220]	December 27 Russian Navy Torpedo boats	The Russians, with four torpedo boats, attacked the Turkish Squadron near Batoum. Two of the boats carried Whitehead "Fish" torpedoes. Both torpedoes ran out of fuel and were picked up by the Turks.	Batoum, Black Sea

---

[215] Sleeman, 336; Greger, "The Origins of Russian and Soviet MTB's", 39-40.

[216] Sleeman, 336

[217] Sleeman, 336.

[218] Sleeman, 336.

[219] Sleeman, 336.

[220] Sleeman, 336.

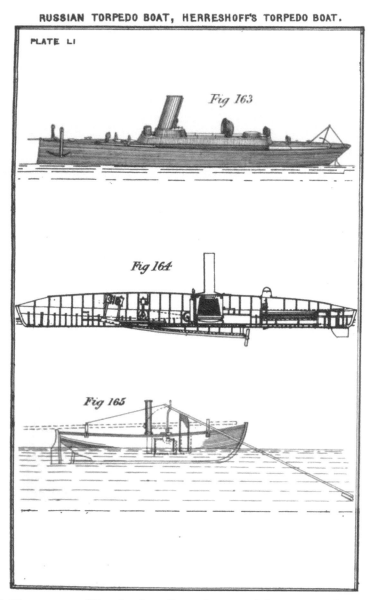

Figure 53. Three types of Russian Spar-Torpedo Boats (Sleeman, 304)

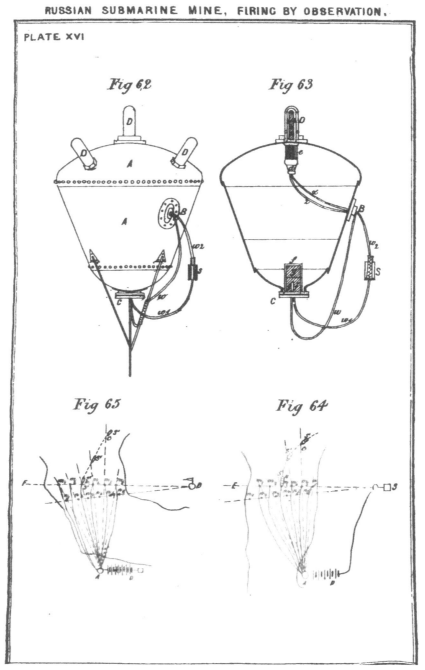

Figure 54. Russian submarine mine fired by contact or observation. (Sleeman, 120)

Figure 55. USN *Wooden Torpedo Boat No. 1,* or *S.S. Stiletto.* The Herreshoff torpedo boat was a great breakthrough in the marriage of technology and craftsmanship. This is the third boat to be a USN No. 1 craft. (U.S. Navy Historical Department)

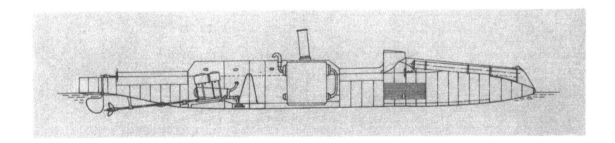

Figure 56. Italian Navy *Nibbio.* (Sleeman)

Date	Craft, Name, Event or Country	Event, Builder and Boat Specifications	City, River, Lake, Sea, Ocean
1877[221]	U.S.Navy *Stiletto*	The U.S. Navy bought a fast steam yacht built by the Herreshoff brothers. *The S.S. Stiletto* is designated as *Wooden Torpedo Boat No.1.* **Speed:** 18.2 knots: **Length:** 95'-0"; **Beam:** 11'-6"; **Draft:** 3'-0", **Displacement:** 31 tons; **Crew:** 15; **Range :** Unknown	Bristol, Rhode Island
1878[222]	January 25 Russian Navy *Chesma*	Two Russian torpedo boats set out to attack Turkish ships and sent two Whitehead "Fish" torpedoes in a Turkish revenue steamer. The Russian Navy had adopted very small MTB designs. They were known as "Minonosk" (torpedo cutters). The boats sank the Turkish guard ship *Initibah.* This was the first successful use of the Whitehead torpedoes. It was the final attack in the Russo-Turkish war (1877-78)	Batoum, Black Sea
1878[223]	Italian Navy *Nibbio*	Italy's first single purpose torpedo boat the *Nibbio* is built by Thorneycroft. The Italians were among the first nations to realize the usefulness of shallow draft, fast, boats to guard their shores.	Italy, Adriatic Sea Tyrrhenian Sea
1878[224]	British Navy *Hull No. 44*	The Herreshoff brothers build their first all steel spar torpedo boats. A separate 2-1/2 hp engine drove the Sturtevant blower for the engine. The first crew called the boat "The Coffin." Mr. G.R. Dunnell of London purchased the boat and gave a demonstration to the Royal Navy on the Thames. The Royal Navy purchased *Hull No.44* and designated the boat as: *H.M. 2nd Class Torpedo Boat No. 63* **Speed:** 16 knots; **Displacement:** 7.5 tons; **Length:** 59' ; **Beam:** 7'-6"; **Draft:** 2'-9"; **Engines:** 1-Compound steam engine, single screw; **Crew:**4	America England

---

[221] Simpson, Richard V, *Building The Mosquito Fleet: The U. S. Navy's First Torpedo Boats,* (Arcadia Publishing, 2001); *Historical Transaction 1893-1943,* 356

[222] Sleeman, 336; Grant, I.A. "The Herreshoff Spar Torpedo Boats of 1878-1880" *Warship International,* 34, No. 4, 1987, 350-355

[223] Fock, Harald. , *Fast Fighting Boats 1870-1945: Their Design, Construction and Use* (Naval Institute Press, 1978), 11

[224] Grant, I.A.. "Herreshoff Spar Torpedo Boats of 1878-80" (*Warship International* No.3, 1977), 259.

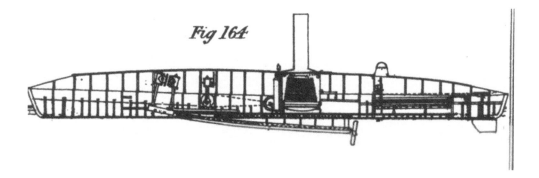

**Figure 57. The British Navy purchased _Hull No.44_ From the Herreshoff brothers
and the British sailors dubbed the new boat "The Coffin." (Sleeman)**

**Figure 58. Feeding the era's coal-fired engines was hard, dirty work. (Library of
Congress Prints and Photographs Division)**

Date	Craft, Name, Event or Country	Event, Builder and Boat Specifications	City, River, Lake, Sea, Ocean
1879[225]	Italian Navy *Avvoltoio*	This was a breathtaking design launched into the modern era of naval warfare. She was rated as a 2nd Class Torpedo Boat, fast and lightly armed. This boat was among the first of this class to carry a "Bow Rudder." **Speed:** 21.3 knots; **Displacement:** 25 T; L:86'0"; **Beam:** 11'-0"; **Draft:** 2'-9"; **Engines:** Compound condensing direct-acting, 2-cyl, 100hp, 1 screw; **Armament:** 2-14" torpedo tubes, one 1-pounder. revolving cannon; **Crew:** 20	Italy
1879[226]	December 11 Herreshoff vs. Thorneycroft Race	The Herreshoff boat was up against the Thorneycroft 2nd Class Torpedo Boat No. 56. The course was 2⅔ land miles. The boats had to start from the tug *H.M. Manly* and from a cold-water start run to Spit Buoy. The finished official resultes were "Thorneycroft: total time from cold, 22min. 21 sec., Herreshoff: 24 min.30 sec." The British boats won the race but the Admiralty liked the rapid starting capacity of the Herrshoff boilers. Herreshoff supplied Thorneycroft with rapid-fire boilers until 1882.	England
1880[227]	April 10 Chilean Navy *Guacolda*	The torpedo *Guacolda* attacked the Peruvian corvette *Union* with two armed, and charged spar torpedoes. One was broken off in a collision with a fishing boat, the other spar charge went off when in came in contact with the boom logs surrounding the ship.	Bay of Callao, Peru
1880[228]	Herreshoff *Hull No. 64*	The Herreshoff brothers made this boat for the Russian Navy. It would influence Russian Torpedo boat design for decades. This would be the last spar torpedo boat the company made. **Speed:** 23 knots; **Length:** 59'-0"; B: 6'-6"; **Draft:** 4'-7", **Engines:** Compound condensing 2-cyl; **Armament:** 4-spar torpedoes.brothers	Bristol, Rhode Island

---

[225] Jackson, 41.

[226] Grant, I.A. 253.

[227] Sleeman, 336.

[228] Grant, I.A. 253-261

Figure 59. The attack on the *Cochran*.

Figure 60. Chilean naval ensign.

Date	Craft, Name, Event or Country	Event, Builder and Boat Specifications	City, River, Lake, Sea, Ocean
1880[229]	April 23 Chilean Navy *Janequeo, Guacolda*	The two spar torpedo boats *Janequeo* (Yarrow) and *Guacolda* moved in to attack Peruvian steam launch. The electrically fired torpedo exploded prematurely causing no damage other than a severe shaking.	Bay of Callao, Peru
1880[230]	May Peruvian Navy	The Peruvians used drifting torpedoes in an attempt to destroy the Chilean blockading ships at the mouth of the Boqueron Channel. The Chilean guard ship discovered the McEvoy drifting torpedoes and destroyed them.	Boqueron Channel, Callao, Peru,
1880[231]	June Chilean Navy *Janequeo, Guacolda*	The *Janequeo* and *Guacolda* make an attack on three large Peruvian gunboats in the Bay of Callo. A mutual explosion of the torpedo sinks one Peruvian gunboat and the *Janequeo*.	Bay of Callo, Callo, Peru
1880[232]	July 3 Peruvian Navy	The Peruvian Navy stepped up the destruction of ships by loading a supply ship with provisions and 300 pounds of dynamite. It was a trap rigged to explode only when the Chileans started to unload the prize provisions. The ship was set adrift and when the Chileans on the *Loa* started the unloading process, it blew, sinking the *Loa* and killing 100 men of the ship.	Bay of Callo, Callo, Peru
1880[233]	October 13 Peruvian Navy	The Peruvians adopted the design of a large framework with 70 barrels of gunpowder from the Confederate Torpedo Department. A clockwork firing mechanism was mounted to a small lighter. The lighter was moored to the anchorage of the Chilean ironclad *Cochrane*. During the night, the lighter drifted out of position and when it exploded with a huge eruption, the ironclad was not scratched.	San Lorenzo Anchorage

---

[229] Sleeman, 336.
[230] Sleeman, 336.
[231] Sleeman, 337.
[232] Sleeman, 337.
[233] Sleeman, 337.

Date	Craft, Name, Event or Country	Event, Builder and Boat Specifications	City, River, Lake, Sea, Ocean
1880[234]	August John Ericsson *Destroyer*	The first public viewing of the *Destroyer* piqued interest around the world. Here at the construction site his ship, Ericsson said, " Ironsides are doomed... we can sink an enemy without ram, steam launch or spar torpedo... " Ericsson's design was about to make a huge impact on naval architecture and naval tactics. Destroyer- Torpedo Gun **Length:** 25'-6"; **Diameter:** 16"; **Total weight:** 1,500 pounds; **Charge:** 300 pounds guncotton; **Range:** 400'-700'; **Speed of charge:** 300' in 3 seconds	Sandy Hook
1880[235]	December 6 Chilean Navy	Three torpedo boats, *Frezia, Guacolda,* and an English Thorneycroft attacked the Peruvian gunboat *Arno.* The ironclad put up a fight and sent a round through the hull of the *Frezia,* which sank her. The other two boats speedily withdrew and the Arno escaped.	Bay of Callo, Peru,
1881[236]	January 3 Peruvian Navy	This was the first use of the newly purchased Herreshoff Torpedo Boat. The boat set out to attack a Chilean ironclad. The ironclad could not be found, and the two towed-torpedoes proved nothing but a hindrance.	Ancona
1882[237]	Imperial German Navy *Schutz* (Defense)	The German designers laid down six 1st class torpedo boats of transverse steel construction, galvanized, with six watertight compartments. These boats were the *Schutz* (Defense), *Flink* (Agile), *Scharf* (Sharp), *Tapfer* (Brave), *Kunh* (Bold), *Vorwarts,* (Onward), *Sicher.* **Speed:** 17.9 knots, **Armament:** 1-3.7cm MG, 2-35cm Bow tube w/4-reloads.	Germany

---

[234] *John Ericsson, A Register of His Papers in the Library of Congress,* Manuscripts Division, Writings File, 1883–1880, Box 5, Reel(s) 5–6, papers 8, 9, 19, 40, 71, 72, 134, 135, 236, 241, 242, 250. *General Correspondence* 1821–1880, Box 4, Reel(s) 4–5. Van Der Weyder, P.H, M.D, Editor. "Captain Ericsson's New Torpedo Boat, *The Manufacturer and Builder* X (No. 10, October, 1878). White, Ruth. *Yankee From Sweden, the Dream and the Reality in the Days of John Ericsson* (Henry Holt and Company, 1960). Barnard, Charles "Ericsson's *Destroyer* and Her New Gun," *Scribner's Monthly Magazine,* XXI, No. 5, (March 1881) 689-693.

[235] Sleeman, 337.

[236] Sleeman, 338.

[237] Fock, 12.

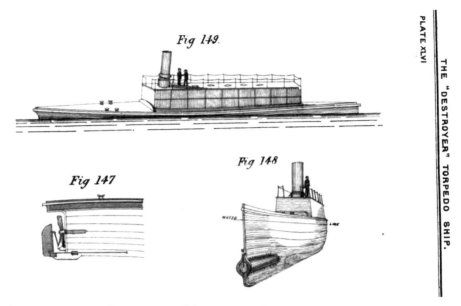

Figure 61. Ericcson's *Destroyer.* (Sleeman, 278)

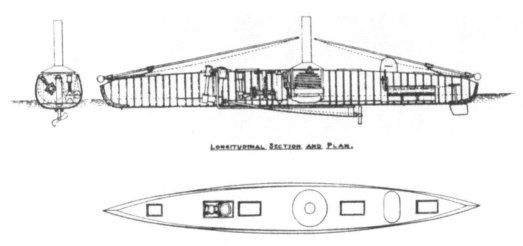

Figure 62. Herreshoff Torpedo Boat made for the Peruvian Navy. (Sleeman, 304)

Date	Craft, Name, Event or Country	Event, Builder and Boat Specifications	City, River, Lake, Sea, Ocean
1882[238]	Japanese Navy *Jeune École*	The Japanese adopted the philosophy of the French *Jeune École* ("young school") and their Diet called for the construction of 48 French designed torpedo boats. This philosophy became the master architect for the Japanese Navy as it designed and built smaller faster ships and deadly torpedo boats.	Japan
1883[239]	British Royal Navy *MTB-85*	The Thorneycroft Yards developed the best-designed torpedo boat in the 1800's. It was a "day boat" which required a "mother ship" for extended operations. The mother ship allowed the crew adequate rest; while they slept, mess, mechanics could work on the boat's engines and rearm and top with coal for the next day's operations. **Speed:** 17.3 knots; **Displacement:** 12.89 tons; **Length:** 19.20m; **B:** 2.25m; **Draft:** 0.46m; **Armament:** 2-Bow Tubes w/ 4-35.6cm torpedoes.	England
1883[240]	Dr. Gustave Laval	The doctor invented the concept of blowing air through slits in the bottom of speedboats to reduce friction and increase speed. This work led to today's modern air cushion and hydroplane craft.	Germany

---

[238] Evans, David C. and Peattie, Mark R. *Kaigun Strategy, Tactics, and Technology in the Imperial Japanese Navy 1887-1941* (Annapolis: Naval Institute Press, 1997), 15.

[239] Fock, 12-13.

[240] Fock, 16.

Figure 63. HMS *2nd Class TB 85.* (Illustration by author)

Figure 64. U.S. Navy sailors getting clothes prior to a prisoner exchange during the Civil War.(Library of Congress Prints and Photographs Division)

Date	Craft, Name, Event or Country	Event, Builder and Boat Specifications	City, River, Lake, Sea, Ocean
1883[241]	Italian Navy *Euterpe* *TB-No.37*	This boat and seven sister boats were built by Thorneycroft for coastal defense. With high speed, shallow draft, these boats could hunt down larger ships in the Adriatic. They were decisive weapons platforms in the Italian-Austro-Hungarian War. Her sister ships were; *Melpomene, Tersicore, Polimnia, Urania* and *Calliop*. **Speed:** 19 knots; **Displacement:** 13.3 tons; **Length:** 63'-0"; **Beam:** 7'-6"; **Draft:** 3'-9"1-Verticle triple expansion engine, 1 screw; **Armament:** 1-25mm MG, 2-14" TT; **Crew:** 9-15,	Italy
1883[242]	Italian Navy *Erato*	The Thorneycroft Yards produced a second design for lightweight class of torpedo boat. This last evolution of designs would greatly influence Italian small craft design for operations in the Adriatic and Mediterranean Seas.	Italy
1884[243]	August 23 Chinese Navy *Young-Woo*	The French introduce its newest design in torpedo boats in the French-Chino wars of 1883-85. The French torpedo boat sank the Chinese frigate *Young-Woo* by a spar-torpedo off shore of Foochow.	Foochow, China
1885[244]	February 15 Chinese Navy *Yu-Yuen*	The Chinese lost the frigate *Yu-Yuen* to two French spar-torpedo boats. The frigate sank in the harbor guarded by heavy gunned shore batteries. This action would move the Japanese to adopt France's naval philosophy and spur close relations in ship construction for decades.	Sheipu, China
1885[245]	July Chinese Navy *Wei-Yuen*	The ship was built as an armed sloop. She later disarmed and designated as a training ship. The Japanese *Torpedo Boat No. 23* torpedoed and sank her at Wei Hai Wei.	Battle of Wei Hai Wei China

[241] Jackson, 139.
[242] Jackson, 127.
[243] Sleeman, 338.
[244] Sleeman, 338.
[245] Evans and Peattie, *Kaigun*.

Figure 65. The Chinese flagship *Yangwu* and the corvette *Fuxing* under attack by French torpedo boats *No. 46* and No. *45*. *Combat naval de Fou-Tchéou* ('The naval battle at Foochow'), by Charles Kuwasseg, 1885. (Wikipedia Commons)

Figure 66. Chinese national ensign.

Date	Craft, Name, Event or Country	Event, Builder and Boat Specifications	City, River, Lake, Sea, Ocean
1885[246]	German Navy 1st Class TB	The Germans brought their plans for their new model torpedo boat to J.S. White & Co., Isle of Wight. These boats were designed to be carried aboard larger ships and were direct predecessors of the fast motor torpedo boats.	
		Speed: 15 knots; **Length:** 37.72m; **Draft:** 2.6m; **Armament:** 1-35cm Bow, above water, 1-3.7cm MG, **Engines:** 1-verticle expansion;	
1885[247]	Imperial German Navy *S-1*	The line of boats *S-1 to S-6* was built by the yards of F. Schichau, Elbing, Germany. At this time, these boats gained a reputation for excellent handling.	Elbing, Germany
		Speed: 19.3 knots; **Displacement:** 84 tons; **Length:** 37.72m; **Beam:** 4.92, **Draft:** 1.07m, fwd, and 2.3m aft; **Crew:** 15; **Armament:** 1-35cm TT; **Engines:** 3-cyl. triple expansion; One Screw; **Range:** 1,400nm @ 10k, 250nm @18k.	
1885[248]	French Navy *Bombe*	The vessels of this class carried three masts and had a ram shaped bow. Much of the vessel was covered in 0.5" armour plate.	France
		Speed: 18-19 knots; **Displacement:** 369 tons; **Armament:** 2-14" torpedo tubes, 4-3 pounder guns, 3 1-pounder revolver guns, **Crew:** 70; **Engines:** 2-vertical expansion; 2 screw	
1885[249]	*Chinese Navy Fu Lung*	The boat was the most modern of the Chinese fleet. It was a steel-hulled, first-class ocean going torpedo boat. The torpedoes were built into the bow and reloading could take place in armour-covered spaces. At the fall of Wei-Hai-Wei the boat was captured by the Japanese and renamed *Fukuryu*.	
		Speed: 18 knots; **Displacement:** 128 T: **Length:** 144'-4"; **Beam:** 16'-5"; **Draft:** 7/-6"; **Engines:** 1-triple expansion, 1 screw: **Armament:** 2-14"TT with reloads, 3-small machine guns.	

---

[246] Fock, 12.

[247] Fock, 14.

[248] Jackson, 56.

[249] Jackson, 169.

Date	Craft, Name, Event or Country	Event, Builder and Boat Specifications	City, River, Lake, Sea, Ocean
1885[250]	November 24 Spanish Navy *Orion*	Germania-Werf in Kiel, Germany built what is considered the best torpedo boat the Spanish navy ever had until they bought German S boats in 1942.	Spain
		Speed: 20 knots; Disp:88 T; **Length:** 37.70m;B: 4.78m; **Draft:** 2.04m; **Engines:** 1,000 hp, 1- Screw; Range: 2,000 nm; **Crew:** 18; **Armament:** 2-356cm torpedo tubes, 2-25mm/42 cal R$V MG.	
1886[251]	July 22 John Ericsson *Destroyer*	The British Admiralty held trials for Ericsson's boat and Torpedo Gun. The *Destroyer* ran a straight course and blew up its target at 300' in 2 seconds. His gun proved viable and the warhead deadly.	England
1886[252]	Spanish Navy *Habana*	The Spanish were very aggressive in keeping a modern fleet of 13 1st Class torpedo boats for its large contingent of ironclads and capital ships. This was the fastest torpedo boat of the era.	Spain
		Speed: 24.5 knots; **Displacement:** 68 tons; **Length:** 127'-7"; **Beam:** 12'-7"; **Draft:** 5'-0" Armament: 2-14"TT Bow mounted; 1-Heavy machine gun; **Engines:** 1 screw, 1-triple expansion eng. **Crew:** 24	
			Spain

---

[250] The Spanish American War Centennial Website. "Spanish Torpedo Boats, First Class." http://spanamwar.com/spantorpedoboats.htm#JULIAN%20...

[251] Barnard, Charles. "Ericsson's *Destroyer* and her New Gun." *Scribner's Monthly* Magazine XXI, No. 5 (March, 1881), 689-693.

[252] Jackson, 214.

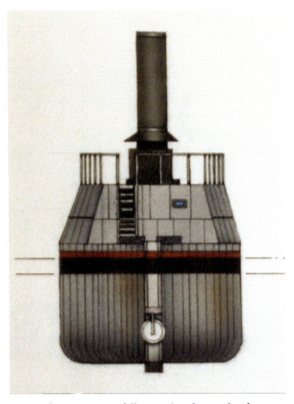

Figure 67. John Ericcson's *Destroyer*. (Illustration by author).

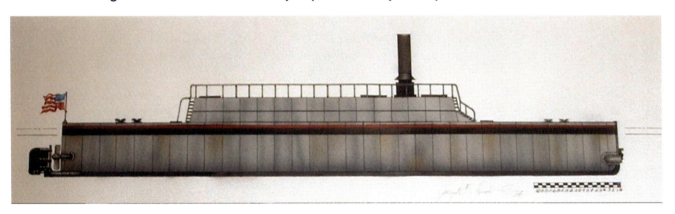

Figure 68. The *Destroyer*, profile. (Illustration by author)

Date	Craft, Name, Event or Country	Event, Builder and Boat Specifications	City, River, Lake, Sea, Ocean
1886[253]	Spanish Navy *Ariete, Rayo,* 1st Class Torpedo Boats	The *Ariete (Ram)* and *Rayo (Ray) were* built by Thorneycroft. The boats set speed records for their day. The *Ariete* made 27 knots in record time. None of the Spanish torpedo boats were not ordered to Cuba and the Spanish-American War. **Speed:** 26 knots; **Length:** 45m; **Beam:** 4,43m; **Draft:** 1.4m; **Armament:** 2-14" Whitehead torpedo tubes, w/2/reloads, 4-42mm Nordenfelt mg; **Engines:** 2 screws; **Crew:** 25	
1886[254]	Spanish Navy *Destructor*	This was one of the first vessels to be fitted with triple-expansion engines. **Speed:** unknown; **Displacement:** 458 tons; **Length:** 192'-6"; **Beam:** 25'; **Draft:** 7'-0"; **Armament:** 5-15" torpedo tubes, 1-89mm cannon	Spain
1886[255]	British Royal Navy *Rattlesnake*	These ships were built to counteract the quickly expanding fleet of torpedo boats being built by many countries. Russia and its large torpedo boat fleet were deemed an immediate threat with the threat of war over Afghanistan. The ship had 19mm (0.75 in) steel protective decks and carried a 102mm gun forward. **Speed:** 19.2 knots; **Displacement:** 550T;**Length:** 200' ; **Beam:** 23' ; **Draft** :10'-4; **Engine:** 2 triple expansion, 2 screws; **Armament** 4-14"torpedo tubes, 1-102mm gun; **Crew:** 66	Britain

---

[253] The Spanish American War Centennial Website, *ibid.*
http://www.spanamwar.com/spantorpodboats1stclass.htm#Azor.
[254] The Spanish American War Centennial Website, *ibid.*
http://www.spanamwar.com/spantorpodboats1stclass.htm#Azor.
[255] Jackson, 274.

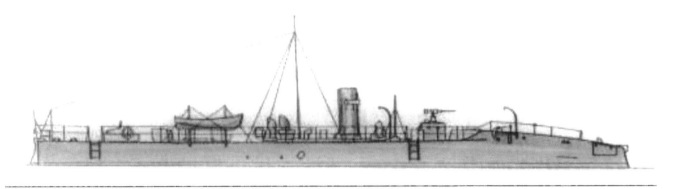

Figure 69. Spanish Torpedo Boat *Habana*. (U.S. Navy Historical Department)

Figure 70. Spanish Navy *Destructor*. (U.S. Navy Historical Department)

Date	Craft, Name, Event or Country	Event, Builder and Boat Specifications	City, River, Lake, Sea, Ocean
1886[256]	France *Balny*	The French Normand shipyards built 10 boats modeled on their highly successful torpedo boat, *TB POTI,* for the Imperial Russian Navy. This version had one major flaw: it rolled badly in high seas. **Speed:** 19 knots; **Displacement:** 66 T; **Length:** 134'; **B:** 11'; **Draft:** 3'-3"; **Armament:** 2-14' TT in bow, two 1-pounder Guns; **Engines:** 1-triple compound, 1-screw **Crew:** 22	France
1886[257]	Russian Navy *Viborg*	This model showed the strong hold that "Old School" navy still had on the ship building industry, worldwide. Even though no capital ship carried sails, the top brass still wanted to put sails on something. This boat was the largest torpedo boat of the period. The Thompson's Yard at Clyde Bank, Scotland, became specialists in this field. The forward bow area had heavy armor plate to the water line. **Speed:** 20 knots; **Displacement:** 169 T; **Length:** 142'-6"; **Beam:** 17'; **Draft:** 7' **Armament:** three 15" torpedo tubes, 2-37mm revolving Hotchkiss cannons, **Engines:** 2-Vertical compound, 2 screw, Three masts w/ sails; **Crew:** 21;	Russia
1888 [258]	Japanese Navy Torpedo Boat *Kotaka*	Japans first torpedo boat is built in England to their specifications. This model would become the forerunner of the torpedo boat destroyer. The hull was built in sections and then shipped to Japan for assembly. This design, while slower then other torpedo boats of the time, did prove that larger torpedo boats could play a major role when they accompanied major warships of the high seas fleets. **Speed:** 19 knots; **Displacement:** 203 tons; **Length:** 164'; **Armament:** 4 1-pounder quick firing gun, 4-14 inch Schwartzkopf torpedos, 2 tubes bow, 2tubes stern	Japan

---

[256] Jackson, 45.

[257] Jackson, 299.

[258] Evans and Peattie, 17.

Date	Craft, Name, Event or Country	Event, Builder and Boat Specifications	City, River, Lake, Sea, Ocean
1889[259]	Italian Navy *Avvoltoio*	The second ship of this name had evolved into a true ocean-going vessel. The ship had the same rigging as a three-masted schooner and could keep up with the fastest of larger ships. They possessed a good radius of action and saw a great deal of service in the Dardanelles against the Turkish fleets.	Adriatic, Black Sea
		Speed: 26.6 knots; **Displacement:** 130 tons; **Length:** 152'; **Beam:** 17'-2"; **Engines:** 2-vertical triple expansion, 2 screws; **Draft:** 7'-9" ; **Armament:** 3-14" torpedo tubes, 2 3-pounder guns; **Crew:** 65	
1889[260]	Russian Navy *Kapitan Saken*	This vessel was by herself considered a threat to her other European neighbors. She had five torpedo tubes (17") in fixed positions; two in the Bows, one in the stern, and two tubes on swivel mounts midships. There were four large caliber guns, two each side on sponsons. Extra loads of torpedoes were carried below the armoured deck and moved into position on small rails.	Baltic Sea
1889[261]	Austria *Flamingo*	This was one of ten small torpedo boats built to offset the advances of the Italian navy in torpedo boat design. They had been based on an earlier successful design of the Schichau boats. She was sunk by enemy gunfire on August 23, 1914, off Pola.	Austria, Adriatic, Black Sea, Dardanelles
		Speed: 19 knots; **Displacement:** 91.4 T; **Length:** 130'; **B:** 15'-9"; **D** 6'-3"; **Engines:** 1- triple expansion, 1 screw; **Armament:** 2-13.8" torpedo tubes, 2-MG	

_____

[259] Jackson, 42.
[260] Jackson, 237.
[261] Jackson, 153.

Figure 71. Imperial Japanese Navy Torpedo Boat *Kotaka*. (Wikipedia)

Figure 72. Austro-Hungarian Navy Torpedo Boat 26 *Flamingo*.

Date	Craft, Name, Event or Country	Event, Builder and Boat Specifications	City, River, Lake, Sea, Ocean
1890[262]	British Navy *Gossamer*	The British built these larger and better-armed boats as a counter to the new threat of the improved French designs. The13 ships of this class came with rapid fire 120mm quick-firing guns mounted fore and aft. The boats were originally known as the *Sharpshooter* class. **Speed:** 19 knots; **Displacement:** 735 tons; **Length:** 230'; **Beam:** 27'; **Draft:** 10'-6"; **Engines:** 2 triple expansion, 2 screws; **Crew:** 91	English Channel, North Sea, Sea of Ireland
1890[263]	U.S.Navy *Cushing TB-1*	The Herreshoff company built their first modern torpedo boat for the U.S. Navy. The *Cushing* was all steel and the design came from the Newport Naval Torpedo Station, Rhode Island. She carried the familiar two bow torpedoes and one on a swivel mount midships. Torpedo reloads came from below decks. Its original cost: $82,750 **Speed:** 23 knots; **Displacement:** 116 Tons; **Length:** 140'; **Beam:** 15'-1"; **Draft:** 4'-10"; **Engines:** 1,720 HP; 2-vertical quadruple-expansion engines; **Armament:** 3-18" torpedo tubes, 3 6-pounderguns; **Crew:** 22	Atlantic Ocean
1892[264]	French Navy *Grondeur*	The boat was a test bed for the newly made Thorneycroft Water Tube boiler. Like the Herreshoff lightweight boiler, it was much lighter and improved speed performance as well as cut down the time between cold boilers to ready to run time. **Speed:** 23.5 knots; **Displacement:** 131 tons; **Length:** 147'-10"; **Beam:** 14'-6"; **Draft:** 4'-6"; **Engines:** 2 triple expansion, 2 screw: **Armament:** 2-14" torpedo tubes, 2-74mm guns; **Crew:** 75; **Range:** Unknown	France

---

[262] Jackson, 196.
[263] Simpson, *ibid.*; DANFS.
[264] Jackson, 206.

Figure 73. The USN's *TB-1 Cushing* was named for U.S Navy Lieutenant John Cushing and his successful attack on the CSS *Albemarle*. (U.S. Navy Historical Department)

DECK TUBE AND PROJECTILE OF A TORPEDO BOAT

Figure 74. Torpedo boats world wide had the disadvantage of always working in the open spaces in even the worst of gun battles at sea. The death toll among these crewmen was always high. (U.S. Navy Historical Department)

Date	Craft, Name, Event or Country	Event, Builder and Boat Specifications	City, River, Lake, Sea, Ocean
1893[265]	February 3-4 Japanese Navy *Torpedo Boat No.6*	Tem Japanese torpedo boats made the first close-in attacks in the East Asian waters on February 3-4 at Wei-Hai-Wei Harbor, China. Swartzkopff torpedoes were used. The boats made several night attacks in freezing weather with the torpedo men suffering from severe frostbite. They hit and sank the Chinese battleship *Tung-Yuan* and the *We Yuen, Sai Yuen, Chen Yuan.*	Wei-Hai-Wei Harbor, China
1895[266]	France Torpedo Boat *Forban*	The Normand Yards built the boat that quickly became known for outstanding performance, open ocean sea-keeping qualities, and the most powerful engines of any torpedo boat in the world. The boat achieved the speed of 30 knots for the first time ever for a torpedo boat. This boat drove the British to step up design and production of Torpedo Boat Destroyers. **Speed:** 30+ knots; **Displacement:** 152 T; **Length:** 144'-4"; **B:** 15'-3"; **Draft:** 4'-5"; **Engines:** 2 triple expansion, 2 screws; **Armament:** 2-14" torpedo tubes; **Crew:** 57; **Range:** 1,000 nm.	Bay of Biscay, English Channel, Mediterranean
1898[267]	Russia Torpedo Boat *Nibord*	This was the first seagoing torpedo boat to run on fuel oil. Later in WWII, the Russians themselves would revert to highly flammable petrol engines for their motor torpedo boats.	Black Sea, Baltic Sea
1898[268]	July 29 British Navy *1st Class TB* TB.28	The Boat was stationed of the waters of South Africa as a training vessel for stockers. The boat ran aground in Kalk Bay, Valsbaai Bay, Cape Town. She was considered a "Construction Total Loss," towed to sea and used as a target ship. Builder: Chiswick, 1886 **Displacement:** 60 tons, **Length:** 129', **B:** 12'; **Armament:** 4-torpedoes	Cape Town, South Africa

[265] Evans and Peattie, 41, 49; Gray, *ibid.,* 150-151.
[266] Jackson, 160.
[267] Greger, *ibid.; Historical Transaction,* 357
[268] Hepper, David. *British Warship Losses in the Ironclad Era, 1860-1919,* (Chatham: 2007), 15.

Date	Craft, Name, Event or Country	Event, Builder and Boat Specifications	City, River, Lake, Sea, Ocean
1898[269]	September 25 U.S Navy *T.A.M. Craven* Torpedo Boat No.10	The boat was named for the Civil War U.S. naval hero Captain T.A.M. Craven, commander of the USS *Tecumseh*. Plans for the boat were provided by the famous French firm, Normand of Le Harve. The boat performed training and experimental work at Naval Torpedo Station, Newport, Rhode island. In 1913, off the coast of Georgia, a boiler exploded, injuring several men and came close to foundering. She was rescued by a tugboat the Estelle and towed through heavy seas to Fort Screven. The old boat was finally decommissioned on November 13, 1913 and then sunk as a target on November 15, 1913.	Atlantic Ocean
1899[270]	Italian Navy Torpedo Boat *Pellicano*	The boat had inherent good sea-keeping abilities but her machinery was never up to the task designed. This was the last heavy torpedo boat that Italy would ever build. She did prove that high speed and maneuverability were essential and a smaller size vessel was imperative. **Speed:** 21 knots; **Displacement:** 183 T; **Length:** 159'-10"; **Beam:** 18'-10"; **Draft:** 5'-0"; **Engines:** Unknown; **Armament:** 2-14"torpedo tubes, 2-37mm guns; **Crew:** 25	1899[271]
1899[272]	U.S. Navy *Dahlgren* Torpedo Boat No. 9	The *Dahlgren* became a class of torpedo boat in the U.S. Navy. Her machinery was much improved over that of the *Craven*. The boat stayed in service as training vessels and during World War I. She was commissioned April 1, 1917, as *Coast Torpedo Boat No. 4,* an escort and harbor entrance patrol boat. She was decommissioned on March 11, 1919. **Speed:** 30 knots; **Displacement:** 146 T:**Length:** 161'-4"; **Beam**: 16'-4"; **Draft:** 4'-8'; **Engines**; 2 triple expansion, 2 screw; **Armament:** 2-18 torpedo tubes, 4-1-pounderGuns; Crew:28	Atlantic Ocean

---

[269] DANFS, I, 3.

[272] U.S. Navy Historical Center. "Dahlgren."
http://www.history.navy.mil/DAFS/Di/Dahlgren-i.htm.
[272] Jackson, 270.

Figure 75. U.S.N *Torpedo Boat No. 9, Dahlgren.* (U.S. Navy Historical Department)

Appendices, bibliography, indexes, and special bonus material will be found in Volume 10.

Printed in the United States
137059LV00002B